Hairdresser Finds Her Roots

The Truth of My Adoption Highlighted a Dark Past

Copyright © 2016, 2021 by Mickee Hicks

All rights reserved. This book or any portion thereof may not be reproduced or used in any manner whatsoever without the express written permission of the author.

"Hairdresser Finds Her Roots:
The Truth of My Adoption Highlighted a Dark Past"

Printed in the United States

Published by Mountain Page Press
Cover design by Meghan McDonald

ISBN-978-1-952714-16-0

First printing, 2016

Additional copies can be ordered through
www.amazon.com and www.mountainpagepress.com

DEDICATION

To all the orphaned children around the world.

To God for always being my strength when I was weak.

Acknowledgements

I would like to thank all those who helped me in my search for my mother; some total strangers, some unforgettable friends.

Mary Eathorne who wrote countless letters to Austria's embassy, other officials in Austria, and the military offices concerning my search for my birth mother.

Leonnie Bomehmer, Independent Searcher in Germany, Austria, and Switzerland. She helps countless adoptees reunite with their birth parents throughout Europe, mostly children who were displaced during World Wars I and II.

Gertrud Matejovic for choosing to give me life. For her sweet spirit and countless years of sorrow after losing her only daughter.

Vera and Lloyd McDaniel for adopting me and giving me a new life in America.

Daniel Bogwicz, my son, who at age ten inspired me to search for truth; the innocence of a young boy asking questions I could not answer till now. Thank you, Daniel, I love you always.

Mary Erickson who helped me to raise money for my trip to Austria to unite with my birth mother. You are my cheerleader and friend.

Robert McDaniel, my adopted brother. You died before your time, may you rest in perfect peace. Your life encouraged me to tell my story, which is yours as well. Even though you were not abused, you suffered in other ways.

To all my **special clients** who supported and stood by me during hard times. I couldn't have made it without your help.

Ruth Anne Uhl, personal historian and coach. You and your company, The Cheerful Word, have been a blessing to me. You inspire so many people in your classes and everyone you meet. Thank you for your love and cheerful heart to help me and others with their family stories; you are a very special person.

I want to give honor to **God**, who helped me through everything that was difficult to handle. You are amazing. Your love never gives up. You opened doors to my history that no man could keep locked. You taught me to forgive when I really didn't want to. You taught me love that I have never known.

Table of Contents

Introduction v
Prologue: My Story 1
Historical Context 7
Who is Gertrud Matejovic? (pt 1) 14
Through a Child's Eyes 21
Hermine's Story 25
Am I Worthy? 31
Young Love Lost 43
The Lockbox, the Cat, and Mom 53
Year of the Search 59
When the Train Pulled into the Station 71
One Year Later 87
Daddy Dearest 91
Who is Gertrud Matejovic? (pt 2)? 107
Trecho 123
Adoption: Provision versus Love 139
Adoption Testimonials 145
Epilogue 163
Appendix 165
Reflections 181
About the Author 187

Introduction

The purpose of this book is to shine more light on adoption issues; to discuss the impact of adoption on the babies born into circumstances such as poverty or war, and those who were raised by parents other than their own birth parents. If you are an adopted child, no matter your current age, or if you are a parent looking to adopt, this book is for you.

Within these pages, you will peer into the life of a teenage mother unable to provide for her infant. This is the true story of a baby born Hermine Anna Matjovic, the natural parents who loved her, and those who became her parents when she was two and a half years old. The story's anchor is Hermine's mother, Gertrud, herself raised by a family in a country devastated by two world wars. Thousands of families were torn by wars that produced killings, rape, starvation, betrayal, lies, and the birth of thousands of illegitimate children who became displaced orphans. Who will really love these children torn from families during and after times of war? Would you? Could you?

Today, thousands of adoptions happen here within the United States as well from war-torn countries. If you are considering adoption, take courage; open your heart with love and compassion to fully understand not only the process but the lifelong effects of adopting a child. Hermine, the child whose story is the focus of this book, was twelve months old when she went into an orphanage. Her mother loved her very much, but she was only sixteen and poor when she became pregnant, seventeen when she gave birth to Hermine. Why are financially strapped parents forced to give up a child? Or why is a child forcefully taken from their mother in a war-torn country? Most adopted children, young or old, feel a sense of being lost, disconnected, and abandoned. Even if they are not told that they are adopted, they feel out of place in families and long for a deep sense of love, belonging, and connection. In my opinion, it is always better to tell children they are loved and were chosen to be part of a family, rather than make up lies or hide the truth of their adoption.

It takes courage to adopt, it takes faith, and it takes a bigger heart than you can imagine to love and raise someone else's child.

I have talked to many people who have chosen to become adoptive parents, and also people who were adopted. The one thing that remains a common experience is the fear of loving and being loved. I'll examine how people define love for an adopted child. For some, love means providing a home, food, education, and a family. For the child, those things mean very little when they don't feel loved or accepted; many feel they never quite fit in. The search for acceptance and love continues throughout their entire lives. On the outside, adoptees can lead a very normal, happy life, but in their moments of sadness or rejection, they reflect on the "What if?" questions that haunt them. Adoptees are always having to explain their adoption to others in social circumstances and to doctors. A constant reminder that they are different.

I would like to encourage truth-telling concerning their birth—helping adopted children to find and give love and,

Introduction

if need be, to find forgiveness, and to discover the real joy of being adopted. With adoption, there is joy and fear, but light will always overcome the darkness if sought after with all your heart. I want to help prepare adoptive parents to answer questions their children will ask—sometimes ponder quietly—and prepare people to hold on to what is good and not to live a life of regrets. It may seem absurd to say, but adopting a child is not the same as adopting a pet! More on this later.

In Hermine's search for Gertrud, will she find what she is looking for? Will the truth of her adoption satisfy her? Come with me on this incredible journey to find the answers to those questions and many more.

I had so many wonderful experiences in my life, many of which centered around doing what I love as a hairdresser. I have started each chapter with a Salon Story to give you a peek inside my life experiences outside my search for my mother. I hope you enjoy each and every one.

Charcoal portrait sketch, Marsha 3 yrs

Prologue: My Story

I would like to take you on a journey. I grew up and had an awesome career, traveled, married and had two children. I divorced after nineteen years and stayed single till I went to Bible college and met my current husband, Kevin. But there is so much in between to tell you.

For the first time, I saw a tiny baby grow and develop a language. My very own baby, John was born on May 19, 1980. Daniel was born on August 2, 1982. They had a natural sense of belonging, they knew at five and six months of age who Mommy was and who the brother was. I was always present in their lives, and up till their teenage years they knew their father. They knew me and I knew everything about them. I adored them and they knew it. I wanted to be as close to them as possible. Feelings of fear would come and go through me during their lives, feelings of abandonment and loneliness, yet love and peace prevailed, it was always constant.

Love was something I struggled with all my life, because I really didn't fully understand it or feel it as a child, but I wanted my children to have it.

My mother never tucked me in at night, read to me, or told me I was loved, but I knew I had to tell my sons, I had to let them know love. I felt such great love for them, love that I never felt in my childhood. I felt a huge duty to protect them, nurture them, teach them, hold them if they cried, and make sure they were educated and knew how to treat others with respect. Things I struggled with growing up, I didn't want my children to struggle with.

I had my share of ups and downs with my kids, much like most families do, but somehow I knew if I could love and overlook their faults, then they would be okay and so would I. The thing I struggled with the most growing up was that I was never encouraged, and never praised. My parents provided for me, but that left me empty inside, searching for the one thing they never provided, love.

Most of my friendships were more like acquaintances. Being raised in the military, we moved a lot, friends came and friends went, no one ever lasted. So after years of that, I never tried to get too close to anyone for fear of having to leave them behind. My second issue growing up was abandonment, I never trusted people. I just knew one day they would just leave me; after all, my birth mother left me in an orphanage.

I was thirty-one when I had my first child and I was scared to death. I was afraid I was not good enough to be a mother; the responsibility was bigger than I was. For nine months, I thought, "How am I going to give this child something I never had, love for the long haul?" The first time I saw my son after he was born, I knew I could love; I was committed to being the best mom I knew how to be. I would just sit and stare at him, sing to him and rock him all day. It was amazing how this small baby boy would be the one to open my heart and bring me love.

He was a handful, but everything good or bad was just a part of love for me, I loved all of it. His first steps, his first words, his hugs, even his crying and all the no's he gave me, it was all a testing of my love. All the things I missed out on when I was a baby. I was my children's cheerleader, I encouraged them in everything. I think I had more fun being their mom than they had with me being their parent.

At thirty-three I had my second son, Daniel. I was ready; I was in love with him before he was born. He was a sweet baby, so cute and so loving and he wanted to be with me and his brother as much as he could. Their dad was like another child, playing and teaching them how to play ball and to be a good sport. We were not the perfect family, but we were better than the family I grew up in.

The first time I spanked my son, it made me cry and feel awful. I remembered how much I was hurt when it was done to me as a child, so I never spanked my boys again. I wanted to teach with love, so I always talked to them about right and wrong ways. Because I was hit a lot, I knew that that it really didn't teach me anything but fear. I never wanted my children to fear me. There are other ways to punish a child and that is exactly what I did. If you were to ask either one of my children what they remember most about their mother, they would say I was always accepting and loving, that I was always on their side and never let them down, I never did forget a promise and I made every occasion fun. I taught them to be honest, loving, and to always treat people with respect. They always knew they were never alone.

"I learned that courage was not the absence of fear, but the triumph over it. A brave man is not he who does not feel afraid, but he who conquers that fear."

– Nelson Mandela

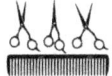

Salon Story

Charlie

During my time in California I met Shonie and Jack. Charlie came from Edgar Bergen's collection of puppets used to entertain friends. Charlie did not appear in Edgar's shows. This story reminds me of so much history that people bring to you in their stories, and sometimes in items they gifted to me over the years. This is one of my favorites.

Shonie was like a mom to me and a best friend, she was always bringing me things and cooking for me and we just had a wonderful friendship. Jack was an inventor who held fifty-five patents. He was brilliant, kind and fun, and I loved them both, but I want to tell you more about Charlie, my most treasured possession.

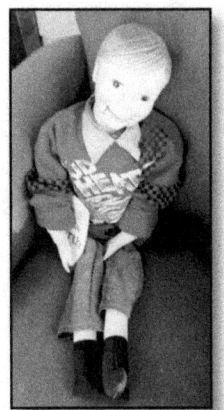

Charlie, 2001

Shonie was married before Jack; her first husband was a furrier for the Italian mob and other seedy characters late in the Roaring Twenties in Chicago, so she was well-acquainted with many of the famous and infamous people of the era. And oh boy, did she have stories to tell.

Many times I visited her home that she and Jack had built. On one visit I saw this adorable puppet sitting on his own chair, like a little king. I asked Shonie what was up with the puppet. She told me that she knew Edgar Bergen and this puppet was one of his that was given to her, and his name was Charlie. I told her if she ever decided to give Charlie a new home, I would love to have him. Shonie loved that puppet.

As the years went by, nothing more was brought up about Charlie. When I told her I was moving to Oklahoma, she cried and hugged me so tight, she really was shaken by the news of me moving. I had known Shonie for over fifteen years by then, and considered her family. The last visit I made, she told me Charlie was ready for a new home and for me to take him. I was floored and excited. I took Charlie and he is still with me today, he even escorted me on a few dates with Kevin. Charlie holds very special memories for me, thank you, Shonie and Jack!

Historical Context

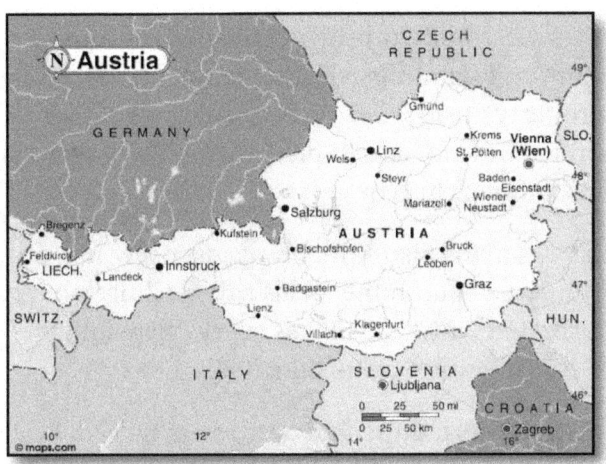

Austria may be a small, landlocked country bordered by Italy, Switzerland, Germany, the Czech Republic, Slovakia, Hungary and Slovenia, but it is rich in history and the arts. It is a tenacious country, having rebuilt successfully from two world wars. Covered in rolling hills, castles, gardens, and home to some of the most delicious food in the world, Austria remains a thriving place to live and visit despite the sorrow of its past. The people there today are farmers, shopkeepers, merchants, and artists known for using every available resource to care for their families. Most families maintain a vegetable garden and are good cooks. Delectable recipes must be woven into their DNA.

Gertrud, my Austrian birth mother, showed me her tiny, thriving garden during my visit to meet her in 1995. Shopping daily at a market for fresh produce is still a viable means to make your meals. In the small town of Ostermiething where Gertrud lives, most people live with very little, but still find joy in many ways. I saw vendors in the streets everywhere—pretzel carts selling the biggest pretzels I have ever seen, most as big as tires! They were so good and fresh, but who could possibly eat a whole one? Not me.

Churches were built long ago with amazing and intricate architecture and paintings, domed ceilings, as well as graves on the property. Inside Gertrud's church was a glass case with a mummified body of a high priest, which was very traditional for the Catholic churches.

I visited Germany also, which was just over the border, where I toured a church the locals called Church of Angels. It was decorated with gold angels everywhere and lots of artwork, it really was hard to take it all in.

The Austrian inns, dotted all over town, have delicious food and interesting décor. I stayed at an inn near Gertrud's home, which had a two-lane bowling alley in it. The lanes were very narrow; the balls smaller than those in the US and the pins were all attached to strings. It was so odd-looking that I just had to play. It was not the same experience as I was used to; there was not much noise when the tiny ball hit the pins, and they never fell down, just dangled from the strings.

In addition to being the birthplace of Wolfgang Amadeus Mozart, and the location for the beloved classic movie, *The Sound of Music*, Austria has a very proud and colorful past.

Between World Wars I and II, Austrians became enamored with German culture. As the birthplace of Adolf Hitler,

Austrians considered identity with the German state a pleasant, if not a temporary alternative to independence. Annexation by Germany provided them with a secure economic position being surrounded by potentially hostile nation-states. But by the late 1930s, World War II put on full display Hitler's failures and the Austrian infatuation with Germany faded. Austria did suffer bombings which caused much ruin of the country's beauty and way of life.

The Allied Forces maintained occupation of Austria after the war until independence removed them from a status of a "belligerent party" that was given during the war. On April 27, 1945, Austrian politicians in Vienna signed the Declaration of Independence. By the end of that year, the Allied Council in Vienna had a democratic parliament again.

It was during this year of transition that American troops, as part of the Allied Powers, occupied Austria. This lasted until 1955.

Austrians initially had great difficulty accepting the assistance of American soldiers during the rebuilding of the country because they had heard only horrible things from the Germans about Americans. Because of their bombing of train yards and buildings as well as concentration camps in Germany, most Austrians did not trust the Americans, and they soon developed a fear and hatred of those who claimed to be working to liberate the Austrian people. After the decades of war they had been through, it was difficult to find trust.

As the soldiers landed and set up kitchens in the town square, the Austrian people got to see firsthand that the Americans were indeed a friendly people—men who knew how to cook, that was a new thing to them. Within days, the children wandered to the square in curiosity and were rewarded with good food shared from the hands of those who proved to be not so evil after all. Slowly people started to trust again. For the rest of the Austrian people, meeting an American soldier quickly became a sign of hope.

As Austria struggled to create a national identity apart from Germany, so did many of its citizens struggle with their identities as everyday citizens. Many had to close businesses and struggled to provide for their families. This struggle for a place in the world was made especially difficult for widowed women and their children. For many years, times were terrible, even unbearable. There was little food and drink for so long that when the soldiers arrived bearing not only food and supplies, but concern and a warm embrace, many women took advantage of this survival kit presented to them.

The children who were born as a result of this time of restoration are estimated to be approximately 1,900 in the city of Salzburg alone and many more went uncounted in Austria. This number represents only the children who were specifically born out of wedlock, having been fathered by American occupation soldiers. There are hundreds of stories of women who were eager to sleep with American soldiers because of their extreme poverty, having finally turned to prostitution for survival. It is a sad fact of any war in history in any country, and a depressing fact of human nature run amok. There was little to offer these children that were a reminder to their single mothers of the horrors of war and the violence that follows.

These infants became wards of the state and resided in displaced persons (DP) camps. DP camps were created by Allied Military Forces to temporarily house the many displaced persons who were forced into leaving war-torn areas. Within these walls was created a special section for babies and young children of the women of Austria. However, many of them have never reunited with either birth parent. Many of these children were adopted out of the country, carrying with them hope for a life absent of strife and poverty in a war-torn country.

While help did come to Austria, the war lasted far too long; the damage was done and it took ten years to restore the country and the people. During the hardship, many committed suicide, many lost family members, and most just tried to pick up their broken lives and rebuild. I think the people primarily have done well now and businesses flourish today. The infrastructure has been rebuilt and the country has once again become a beautiful place. I did visit many of the places that still remind us of that time in history, but for the most part, it is a thriving and beautiful country. I long to go back.

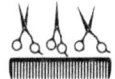

Salon Story

In Carmel, California Anything Can Happen

I was ready for my day to start and my appointment book was full. As I greeted my first client, I was in my zone and the day went well from there. After lunch I saw a new name on my book, Phyllis Coates. She asked for me but I didn't know her or who she was. In came this beautiful, small, slender woman who looked like a movie star. Only five feet two inches tall, she lit up the room with her cheerful smile and deep voice. We chatted and I started doing her hair. She said I was recommended to her because I had worked in Beverly Hills. She told me she was doing an interview in LA next week and needed me to do her hair like her portfolio pictures for the studios. Now I was more than interested in her identity.

I figured out quickly that she was someone special who I wanted to know, but I never guessed in a million years who she really was. We really hit it off chatting away when I learned that she was the second Lois Lane from the original Superman series on TV.

We became fast friends and did all kinds of fun things together outside the salon. I went to lunches with her and met her friends. I went to her house and helped her move.

She gave me signed pictures and even appeared in a hair video I did for advertising. She is an amazing woman and I am so glad I am her friend. She also brought her dog to the salon, leaving him in the car after introducing us—his name was Lucky because he was a rescue dog. Lucky is a very happy dog.

Who is Gertrud Matejovic? (Pt 1)

Gertrud Matejovic

Gertrud Matejovic was born in March of 1932 in Salzburg, Austria. World War II was brewing in their neighboring country, Germany, and began in 1939.

Gertrud's parents, her Bosnian father and Austrian mother, had survived WWI (1914-1918) and they were familiar with the tremendous cost of war, not only in human life, but economic devastation for the country. They were average farmers; they owned cattle and raised produce. They were still recovering from the first World War when WWII pushed Gertrud's family deep into poverty, with little to eat. Some of her family members and many neighbors were killed in the fighting. In 1940, at eight years old, fear became a part of daily life for Gertrud and her family.

Little else is known about her family, except that Gertrud had a sister, a mother who couldn't care for her children after WWII, and a father who became an alcoholic, and later killed himself after suffering from severe depression, another casualty of war. Gertrud's sister was three years older and married a local German soldier, looking for hope and security in a war-torn country. As was the case after WWI, after WWII, Austria, like many countries, was once again in need of military assistance.

In 1944, American troops were sent to help rebuild the country. Young girls looked at the American soldiers as caretakers who could take them away from the poverty, loss, death, and destruction of their country. Most women had little education unfortunately, and during and after every war, prostitution became a way of survival for hundreds of thousands of women and girls, some as young as eleven. As in so many war-torn countries, people will survive any way they can. It becomes a desperate way of life.

Neighbors helped one another as much as they could, but money was in little supply. Gertrud's neighbor wanted to help her by giving her an education. At fourteen, she was put into a trade school so she could earn money and not have to struggle or take up the street trade as the war was coming to an end. She learned the art of glassblowing and weaving so she could make and sell her art as a street vendor. With little education, that was all she could hope for and it brought her only the barest of income; not enough to help her family. People were starting to rebuild their lives any way they could.

By the time the American forces arrived in 1944 to help reconstruct the country, Gertrud discovered another way to survive. She had a friend, Linda, who worked in a pub/restaurant with boarding rooms on the second and third floors.

Who is Gertrud Matejovic? (Pt 1)

Linda got Gertrud a job as a waitress and a room to stay in. At fifteen years old, Gertrud's mother told her she could no longer support her and did not stop her from leaving home.

Now a fully independent young lady, she observed many soldiers who came in and out, both at the pub and the rooms. They were spending money, lots of it, every day. She was a virgin and afraid she might be solicited by the men that came in. But she was also intrigued at the same time. She preferred to remain cautious, serving them food and drinks, charming them with her wonderful personality hoping for generous tips and perhaps even meeting one that might take her to America. Gertrud dreamed of a big future for herself. She knew being a woman meant she would get attention and no one needed to know she was only fifteen years old; in fact, age was never part of the discussion.

Linda her only friend, was a prostitute by the age of sixteen. Now twenty, she tried to recruit Gertrud, but at such young age, Gertrud was not interested.

Gertrud's story develops as Hermine is born. More about Gertrud later.

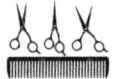

Salon Story

Barber Shops and Shopping Carts

In Monterey, California I was working in a barber and styling shop; the men on one side and two women on the other. The men were always coming in without appointments and the women had to have appointments, so there was constantly foot traffic. The barbers cut up a lot, told jokes, talked about sports and manly stuff, often very loudly. Kids often came in with their dads. One particular day, this mom brought in her two and a half year old in a shopping cart. I thought, how cute, till she asked if anyone would cut her son's hair. It was his first haircut, he was not really excited to be there at all and I could feel a scream coming on from this child.

I stepped in and said, "I will cut his hair," and asked if the mom could bring him to my chair. She said no, he wouldn't get out of the shopping cart; I would have to cut his hair in the cart.

Really? How strange; but sure enough, every time we tried to get him to sit in the chair, he would start screaming. So I brought the shopping cart in, and I cut his hair in the cart. Trying to get all around him was challenging to say the least.

Oh by the way, he didn't want the water sprayed on him either. Believe me; I needed a glass of wine after that cut. The mom thanked me and I thought I would never see them again but they became very good customers, shopping cart and all. Who knew?

Through a Child's Eyes

Taken from my mother at one year of age, I was put into an orphanage full of strangers and left for eighteenth months.

But let me back up a minute and start from the beginning. As far back as I can remember, my mother visits me but never comes back to take me home. I don't know why.

At two and a half years old, I was adopted, my name was completely changed, and I was removed from my country and sent to live with strangers in America, thousands of miles from home. I am then given a brother, Robbie, who is six months younger than me whom I never knew before. In my new house, English is spoken, even though all I knew was German. I knew who to call mommy, though there was no daddy or sibling until I was taken to America. It was so sudden; everything was taken away from me and replaced. Where is my mother? This is a scary place. I used to be called Hermine, but these new people call me Marsha.

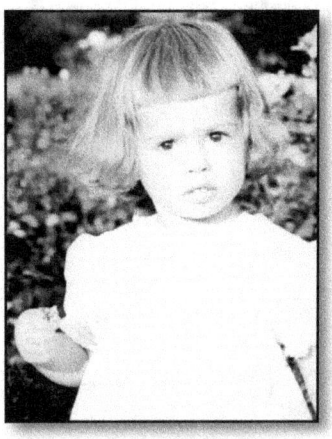

Marsha, 3 yrs, US 1953

And Marsha was my name until 1996. I chose to give myself the new legal name of Mickee at forty-seven years old to finally rid myself of all the memories of my past life as Marsha.

Robbie & Marsha, 1954

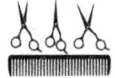

Salon Story

A Beauty School Oops

Beauty school was mostly learning theory and working with mannequins. For the last five months we were able to go on the floor to work on real customers. I was very excited to finally graduate and start my career as a hairdresser; I was going to get paid for my first haircut! We always had a teacher watching and hovering over us.

My first haircut was a woman with very long hair; she wanted a shorter style and brought a picture. I was so nervous I had to excuse myself at first. I ran into the bathroom in tears, thinking, "What if she hated what I did, what if it turned out badly." I made myself nuts.

I composed myself and went back out. We talked about what she wanted before I began, and all through the haircut. Things seemed to be going well. But, when I was done the customer cried. She wanted her hair back; she said it was too short. I was so embarrassed.

The instructor came over to check the cut and calm things down. She said it was a perfect cut and the customer really wasn't sure what she wanted, but I had done what she asked. Both of us cried, but once the hair is on the floor, it is gone for at least four years to get the length back that she came in with. It was the worst first day I ever had! The truth is, hair always grows back.

Hermine's Story

I was born into pretty normal family circumstances with a mother and a father. Both were present at my birth. I went home and both parents were there to raise me. I guess I was cute—I got kissed a lot and felt loved. Life was just starting for me, but ending for my parents.

When I turned one, my mother took me on a ride. I had a small suitcase, and was just learning to walk, so Mommy helped carry me and my bag. I loved to ride in the car with Mommy. Mommy spoke German and some English and Dad spoke mainly English. So I guess I was becoming a bit bilingual right from the start. My hair was very short and straight, Mommy kept it gently combed.

I didn't know there were problems between Mommy and Dad, but it seems there was. Dad was gone a lot, Mommy said he was working a lot, and his job caused him to travel. Mommy stayed home with me, she wasn't working. She was very young, only seventeen, and Dad, he was much older, more like a grandpa, but I called him Da Da. Soon after my first birthday, on that road trip I told you about, I found myself in the parking lot of a Catholic-run home for orphans, or as my records indicated, displaced persons. Mommy took me by my hand, helping me walk inside to a big room full of other children and nuns. It seemed like we were there for hours. The nuns took me into a dining room where kids were eating. I was told to sit down and eat with them, that Mommy would be right back, but Mommy never came back.

It was almost one week before I saw Mommy again. She came to see me but I thought she was coming to take me home. I was confused, why was Mommy visiting me and not taking me home? I cried when she left and looked for her to return.

Every week she came and played with me and hugged and kissed me but every week she would leave me there. Was I a bad child and Mommy had to leave me in an orphanage? I started to get very quiet, not wanting to play or eat. I just sat there most of the time trying to figure this out in my very small, underdeveloped mind.

After I turned two, Mommy came less and less. By now I was talking and walking and I asked a lot of questions but didn't get many answers. After being there for one year—with strangers coming and going, and very strict nuns—no one could tell me when Mommy was coming to take me home. I guess I didn't expect she was coming to take me home ever again, yet I didn't know why.

Lloyd & Vera, Illinois circa 1954

By the time I was two-and-a-half, I never saw my Mommy again. I longed to see Mommy one more time and ask her why she left me. Why did she not want me anymore? Was I bad, or too much trouble? I just didn't know and it made me very sad.

The boat we were on to America was huge; a lot of

people were on board. I knew no one. It took a few days to get to America, and really, the boat was kind of fun. People seemed nice and other kids would play with us. Mom told everyone that Robbie and I were adopted. I didn't know what that really meant. All I knew for sure was my mommy wasn't with us.

I tried to be positive and look for every opportunity to ask where Mommy was, but after a few months, I stopped asking. It was obvious I had a new life without her. We moved a lot, it was part of the military life to move every two or three years, so I was always meeting new kids, going to new schools and living on bases in different houses. I didn't make close friends because I knew I was going to leave and didn't want to be sad like I was when Mommy left me.

Fred, Lloyd (holding Marsha),
Vera, Freddie
Vera's mother (holding Robbie)
IL, circa 1954

I started to live in a pretend world, a world of, "What ifs?" I made up stories about who I was and where I was from. Life to me just didn't seem real.

Robbie, my new brother, was also with new parents, he was very quiet and he rocked back and forth all the time, making a humming noise. He seemed more confused and sad than I was. I could tell my new mom was concerned about him, because she would hold him, cuddle him, and kiss him a lot, and didn't have much to do with me except discipline. I guess Robbie was more lovable than me.

As I grew older, it got harder. The lady I had to call mom

was mean to me, and not at all like Mommy. I was always in trouble about something, getting punished, spanked, or beat. I fell deeper and deeper into despair, I hated being different. My mom was always telling me how grateful I should be that she took me in when no one wanted me. She always introduced me as her adopted daughter, never simply her daughter. Robbie became her special project, he pretty much had her wrapped around his little finger, and he could do no wrong in her eyes. He never got a licking or punished.

Dad became more distant too; he pulled away and grew farther away from his feelings. He began to do all the spanking and beatings; he did whatever Mom said. She called me a liar and a troublemaker all the time till one day I believed it. I had temporary friends and they treated me really good, but when I got home, there she was making up stuff to tell Dad so I would get a beating. This continued till I was about fifteen, too old to spank, but I still got punished and ridiculed. I was convinced that Mom hated me. Robbie, well he never had many friends. He was very distant and preferred being alone, but he was very smart and aced all his tests while I failed most of mine. At fifteen years old, I was miserable with my family and still had no answers to why I had to leave Austria.

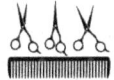

Salon Story

Gift on Rodeo Drive

It was 1976, and I was working in Beverly Hills which was an amazing place to work. I met many celebrities and other interesting people. It was the year I married my first husband, the father of my two boys. I was making good money but weddings are expensive, even small ones like the one I was planning.

We had moved from Florida to California at the end of 1974 and I immediately made fast friends and customers, people much wealthier than I had ever been around before. I wanted to get married in North Carolina where my mother was because I felt the need to honor and include her in some way in my life. I was always trying to bond with her. Meanwhile, at the salon, a huge box came from Hawaii. It was a dress, an amazing dress with a simple card that read, "Please accept this gift; I want you to have a beautiful day as a bride."

I was shocked. The customer who sent it called and asked if the dress arrived and had I tried it on. I said yes, it was amazing and I was at a loss for words. She told me she delighted in surprises and her seamstress would come over to see if it needed any alterations.

I was the talk of the salon. She also wanted to know about flowers, I told her I was getting married in North Carolina not California, so she just gave me a credit card for the flowers. It was like she got joy from giving to others more than receiving. I learned a lot from her about giving unconditionally. She was amazing and I looked great too.

AM I WORTHY?

This question has haunted me most of my life.

As a child, knowing I was adopted, I knew I had to be someone special—that's what my father told me. Yet I never felt special, I felt more like I was a mistake and these people felt sorry for me because I was an orphan. I was two and a half years old when I was adopted, very young, yet I knew who my mommy was, and I knew somehow that she didn't come with me to America. And I knew I had a new mother, a brother and a dad too, an entirely new family that I didn't know.

I didn't fully understand why I had to leave my natural mother or the orphanage and I had a difficult time relating to my new family, but I knew one thing for sure, I better measure up or I could be left again. I was always afraid that this family would tire of me and I would have to go with another family.

I think at some time or another, everyone questions their worth and value. I certainly did. My mother

Marsha, Fayetteville, NC 1965

would say, "Proper girls do this and good girls do that, and ladies do things this way." I was constantly trying to be whatever Mother wanted me to be in fear that I could be shuffled off to another family if things didn't go well.

As I got older, I tried to be what Mother wanted, but she always found fault with everything I did or said, it seemed like nothing I did was the correct way. Both Mom and Dad had strict rules and harsh punishment if those rules weren't followed. I wanted to please them both but I always felt like a failure, and was told so often.

My brother Robbie was the smart one. It seemed like he was favored because he got excellent grades in school with little studying, and I struggled just to get Ds. I later found out I was dyslexic, a condition millions of people have, but I didn't know anything about it until I was an adult. I was constantly called stupid, slow, not smart, and lazy. You name it, I was called it. My parents didn't know about dyslexia or such issues like mental illness or depression. It just wasn't talked about. In those days, we had to present ourselves as one big, happy, normal family. In the military we had an image to live up to. We were to be viewed as an Ozzie and Harriet type of family; no matter what went on at home, it was to stay behind closed doors.

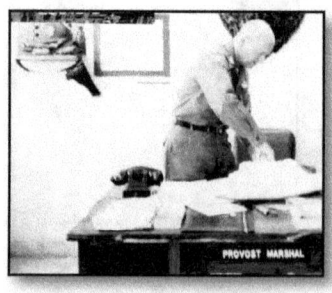

Lloyd as Provost Marshall
Fayetteville, NC circa 1968

In the last years of service to his country, Dad was the Provost Marshal at Fort Bragg and a full-bird colonel in the army (also known as full colonel).

Mom was on every committee that came along. She was constantly hosting events, which became a major focus in her life.

My parents were the ones others looked up to. So if we failed, it reflected on their parenting. We were taught to dress well, have good manners, respect the rules, and to always act appropriately in public. To them, there were two ways to do things, the right way and the wrong way, no gray area. No excuses or arguing, what was right was always right, wrong was always wrong, and harsh punishment a way of life. I tried to stay away from getting punished or bringing shame to my parents, but I seemed to fail all the time in their eyes. Even if I told the truth, Mother would call me a liar. When my grades were bad, she called me stupid and yelled at me for not trying or being lazy, telling me that Robbie made good grades and I should too. Having dyslexia and not knowing about it till in my twenties, I did feel stupid and like a failure, just like Mother said. So as I got older, I did feel unworthy, not loved, and not valuable at all. I had friends and I was extremely social, but somehow that was never enough, I wanted my parent's approval. I never got it.

After Dad died at the young age of sixty-two, I didn't care anymore about what my mother thought of me. But I still wanted to do what was right, and constantly looking out for her became a full time job after I discovered she had Alzheimer's disease. Now I had to help someone I didn't like and I knew she didn't like me either, but I did it anyway because it was the right thing to do.

She lived seven years with that disease and in the end she didn't know my name or anything about me, except the one thing she would tell everyone: that her adopted daughter was the cause of all her troubles. Her constantly pointing that out to me did not exactly bring me joy and coincided how I already felt about my life and failures. In my heart, I just wanted to run away and not care about this woman who had brought me to America and treated me so harshly, But I knew in my spirit I had to do what was right; even if I didn't want to, it seemed better than living in quiet shame.

I had Mother placed in a nursing home where she was well-cared-for. I called every week, checked on her and paid what Medicare didn't cover monthly. The caretakers told me she was mean and hateful to the staff, so they asked if she could have a glass of wine to calm her. I said, "If you think it is okay for her to drink, but only one glass in the evening please." Of course she was taking medication but somehow she still acted in abusive ways.

I saw her only a few times in the seven years she was there, and each visit was worse than the previous. After about three years I stopped going because of her violent outbursts. I wrote letters that they read to her and I called weekly, but after a while she forgot her life, past and present, and only remembered her hate for me. That was so upsetting for her and me.

At the end of her life, she was taken by ambulance from the nursing home to the hospital, badly dehydrated, and things only got worse. Mother suffered a heart attack, deteriorated quickly, and was put on life support. It was two weeks before a doctor called to me to tell me she was on life support with no hope to live. She was brain-dead and they needed my permission to disconnect. The doctor spoke to me in a very uncaring way which I thought was odd. I proceeded to tell her that I was never informed about Mother's condition and didn't even know she was taken to the hospital. Then the doctor calmed down and started to tell me everything. Mother had been in the hospital a little over fourteen days and only talked about her awful daughter.

The doctor told me it was time to discontinue life support for her, it was the kindest thing I could do for her in the condition she was in. So I did give the doctor my permission.

It was so difficult making such a final decision. I thought if she was dead, she could no longer hurt me or struggle with her own hateful emotions toward me, but as time went on, the hurt in my heart was still there.

After she died, I went to the hospital to sign papers and get her things and a nurse came and said to me in a high pitched voice, "You're the daughter?"

"Yes," I said.

"Your mother spoke awful about you and how you were the cause of all her problems. She said that you were an awful daughter and she wished you had never come with her to America."

Wow, I was stunned; I had no idea that in her condition that she could say such awful things. I told the nurse and doctor that all my life she saw me as a failure and unworthy; she did adopt me but never loved me or accepted me. I couldn't believe as Mother lay dying that her hate for me was still so very deeply rooted. I explained that I never fully understood my mother's hate toward me, that I tried to be a good daughter, but in her eyes, I never had a chance. The nurses seemed to understand but it did make everyone sad for us both. Unworthy of her love, that was me.

Vera's Funeral

As my dad's casket was being unearthed to place Vera's ashes on top, I sat and watched with little emotion, asking God why it had to be like this. Why did both parents die without me being there? Why was I so unimportant to them? I was truly having a pity party for myself.

No one came for a funeral, no church services, not even anyone from the care facility, just me, my husband, and my two boys, ages five and seven. My younger son asked me, how did Grandma get into that small box? I chuckled and realized he knew nothing about cremation. I tried to explain the best way I could without scaring him. We threw dirt on the grave, said a prayer and that was that, all over. I thought all my troubles and misery were over now that she and Dad were dead, but I was wrong; in the years to come I was angry, hurt, and mad that I did not get the last word. I felt robbed of my feelings not being heard by them. I still had questions and no answers.

I wanted my parents buried together so I had Dad's grave dug up. As my dad's casket was being revealed, I paused to take a long look at it, and memories flooded in, good and bad. Then Mom's box of remains was placed on top with him. I had no tears for her, I was numb. I felt bad that I couldn't even cry. Yes, I felt I was a failure as a daughter and I struggled to be a good wife and mother in my own life. But I really believed that when Vera died my troubles would all be over and buried with her.

The truth is, it wasn't the end; the scars were still visible, the failed childhood filled with disappointment and shame stayed with me a long time. About nine years later when my marriage was falling apart, I struggled to keep hanging on, but it slipped away after nineteen years. All that was left was another failure. Once again I heard my mother's voice: "You will amount to nothing, you can't do anything right, you're so stupid." I tried to keep my marriage, but after filing bankruptcy and being sued, my house had a lien on it. My bank account was frozen by the IRS from the things my ex did without my knowledge, and I felt pretty beaten down. My husband had borrowed against our house from a loan shark without my knowledge, forging my signature. I lost the house that we had lived in for ten years, my beauty salon, as well as my marriage because of that loan shark and my husband's bad business dealings. I was as low as I could get. No money, no salon to earn an income to support my kids and no place to live. I was at an all-time low in my life, but I knew somehow we could get through it all. I was determined and I did have the support of friends, church and my loyal customers.

One of my customers, Gloria, told me she and her husband had talked it over and she had to help me, so they built me a small salon in one of the buildings they owned. They were wealthy and owned several properties. She saved my butt. Thank you, Gloria; I finally felt loved and worthy.

The salon was small, about 150 square feet, but in a very good location, and they built the shop just the way I wanted it. I didn't have to pay rent for six months, and then after that I would pay something I could afford, no pressure. I got a small rental house nearby and the kids and I moved in. I told my ex it was time for him to go and for us to divorce. He refused to work and had put me and the kids through financial destruction. I failed at that marriage but I did learn another side of myself, the survivor; I was much stronger than I thought. I could climb back and with the help of my loyal customers, friends, and my church, I had a new life. The church paid my utility bills, gave me groceries, and helped me with necessities for the kids. Everyone seemed to want to help me, yet my parents never saw this worthiness in me. Wow, it felt so good to be loved and cared about.

I started to work harder than ever to make sure my sons had what they needed, yet somehow I seemed to begin failing at parenting. The love was always there and my kids loved me too, but I was working so much, I wasn't keeping up with what they were involved in and who they hung out with. I really felt separated from them.

My oldest son dropped out of school after his junior year, and he started keeping bad company. I learned much later--when he was arrested--that he was involved with drugs. I also found out later that he is bipolar and that it caused further issues I could do little about. There is no cure for this, only medication. I prayed for him and loved him but I wasn't able to help him very much.

My other son, Daniel, dropped out in his junior year as well and he thought it was his job to look out for his brother. He didn't want to do drugs, but he didn't want to do much with his life either. I left the apartment we lived in and I moved out feeling like a failure as their mother. Things had gotten so out of control.

I moved in with a friend and checked up on the boys daily and paid their rent. Things were not good but I didn't know how to help them and work to support all of us. My older son's drug use got worse and so did his behavior, but Daniel stayed to help him. It was a bad situation for us all.

I was desperate for help and that is when a friend came to me and got me into a women's Bible study; that really changed my life. I could see things more clearly and I started to forgive myself and make better choices. Before this time, I attended church, but this was my first experience at a deeper level building relationships not only with women, but with God and my life.

The situation with my older son got worse. Drugs and bad company got him evicted from the apartment, leaving my younger son Daniel with no place to live. I rented a room in a friend's house, but she didn't want to take my son in, so I made a small place in my salon for him, with a sleeping bag on the floor and a bathroom; it was all I could do at that time. Daniel was glad to be in a safe place.

Daniel had no car and no way to support himself and was soon turning eighteen. I felt I needed to do something, but I wasn't financially able to provide a home for us both. After losing everything and not ever receiving child support, I was strapped for money and could not get us a home together.

Daniel is an amazing young man. He never complained about staying at the salon, and he really tried to find a place to live with friends. I was with him and provided food and what I could, but I had to work and he had to roll up his bed early and look for work while I worked. After several months of prayer, I decided to move and enroll at a Bible school in Tulsa, Oklahoma. I knew people who had attended that particular school and felt like I should either commit and go, or stay and find a home for us. I talked it over with Daniel and he said he wanted to go with me and help me, he was ready to leave and so was I. I was thrilled that I was going on this journey and to have Daniel with me made it even better. I had to leave my older son behind where he was safe in a hospital being treated for his bipolar disease. I had signed papers for him to be kept there for his own safety. So a new start was coming.

My sense of worthiness was just budding, and the changes that came about from that faithful move were nothing short of life-affirming. More on that adventure later.

Music inspires me and lifts my soul. A song by Whitney Houston, The Greatest Love of All, and others who sing about how cherished our children are and how we, as adults, should learn from their childlike hearts—how we need to see ourselves as important people to look up to for all children. They don't need heroes who are athletic or famous, their heroes should be you and I, living and loving and showing them the way through life, right in our own homes. They will gain strength and courage from our examples, even when we inevitably fail. We teach them they too, can get back up and live and love fully after mistakes are made.

Side note: Learning to love yourself is a gift. I know God will always love you and I believe He has been with me through my whole life. There is strength in love.

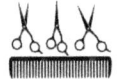

Salon Story

Birth and Beauty Come Together

In my salon in Oklahoma, I was fixing a woman's hair and it was obvious she was very pregnant and close to her delivery date. As I was cutting her hair, I asked, "So when are you due?"

She replied, "Right now, my water just broke, oh my goodness."

I went into panic mode. "Call an ambulance!" I yelled.

She was having rapid contractions and started yelling, and we laid her on the waiting room couch, holding her till help came. It was the longest five minutes of my life. The baby came just as the EMTs arrived. Whew, that was close. She did come back to finish her haircut in a few weeks.

Young Love Lost

I was nineteen when I was pregnant with my first child. I was living with a female roommate and her three-year-old son from a broken marriage where her husband had committed suicide after returning from Vietnam. I met a wonderful man on the base at Fort Bragg, a man who was ready to serve his country in wartime. Jack was good looking and very loyal to his military duties. I never met his parents, but they had to be wonderful people. We dated for five months and Jack told me his unit was being shipped out in a few weeks. He wanted me to wait and keep writing him, he said he would be coming back for me and he wanted to marry me, he even gave me a ring. I was excited and afraid for him going so far away to fight a war we should have never been in. I had lived on a military base all my life. I know the hazards of war, how it tears families apart and how some young men return suffering PTSD, become a high risk for suicide, or worse, just return home in coffins. This was an experience I didn't wish on anyone, especially Jack.

I didn't hear from Jack for a month or so after that tearful goodbye but I thought about him daily. That last time we stayed together we held onto each other all night while making plans to see each other again; he was so tender and caring. We had only known each other a few months before he had to leave, but to me it seemed like we knew each other well enough to stay committed to the relationship.

The first letter I got was wonderful, full of love and sadness, Jack was willing to share everything with me, all his emotions and himself. I loved that about him. Jack told me he wanted to marry me and I told my parents I was engaged. They were not thrilled or supportive and said very little. I was on my own and I didn't need their permission, but I did seek their blessing. I had a good job and I was content not to date while Jack was gone and stayed busy at work. Our letters were coming and going pretty regularly; Jack told me he had made plans for rest and relaxation (R&R) time. After five months he could get two weeks off and he was going to bring me to meet him in Hawaii to get married.

I was more than excited, I started planning right away. But it seemed apparent something wasn't right. I am very regular with my menstrual cycle and one month I didn't have a period, but thought nothing about it, until the second month rolled in and still no period. I was scared that I was pregnant but didn't want that to be true. My roommate and very good friend said she would stand by me and help in any way she could, but I knew I couldn't handle raising a child without being married and I didn't want to show up in Hawaii pregnant. How was I going to tell Jack? So I didn't.

I wasn't showing yet but I was in the last week of my fourth month when I got a letter from Jack's mother telling me Jack was killed by friendly fire. Jack would not be coming home, ever; his mother told me. There would be no wedding in Hawaii.

Oh my God, how is this possible? I just couldn't believe what I was reading. Jack is dead, no wedding in Hawaii, and no father for my unborn child. And if my parents found out I was pregnant and not married, I would catch their wrath too. Overwhelmed with grief, I just shut myself in my room for days crying and trying to decide what to do.

My roommate said to me, "Can you abort? Would you consider it? That way no one will ever have to know." And the more we talked, the better abortion sounded. One of Jack's friends offered to pay for it, and at that time it was illegal, so we would have to find a clinic that would do it. We found an underground place and made arrangements to drive from North Carolina to New York in the middle of the night to get the abortion early the next morning and drive back before anyone missed us.

I didn't know what to expect. I just knew I wasn't going to have a child outside of marriage. I was just over four months, I wasn't showing and I felt if I was going to do it, I had to do it now. My friend and I drove ten hours and checked into a cheap motel near the underground clinic. We got up early after only a few hours of sleep.

I was told not to eat the morning of the procedure, so at 6:00 a.m. we checked into the clinic where a large nurse dressed in white came out to greet me. The room was cold, very clinical, and the nurse was not very friendly. She asked me a bunch of questions and I signed permission for the abortion and paid the money up front, it was all business. And then I waited about forty-five minutes to be called in. As I was waiting, I could hear yelling and crying and saw young girls being wheeled by on their way to a recovery room.

The nurse came out and told me to follow her, get undressed and put a gown on and lay on this table with my feet up in the stirrups. The room was very cold and had no pictures or decorations on the walls, just an exam table and a tray of instruments. The nurse administered the anesthesia and I got numb in my lower back pretty quickly. I was so scared and felt so alone.

The doctor came in and explained the procedure. I will never forget it, he said, "After you are medicated but still conscious, I will insert a tube in your uterus attached to a suction machine that will be like a vacuum to suck out the fetus. This will only take a few minutes and then we will clean out the uterus. Then you will need to rest and drink water. You will have a heavy flow of blood for a few days and cramping, but do not be concerned, it will stop."

They brought in the equipment and soon I was attached to it. I was not under a heavy-enough medication because I felt a lot more pressure and pain when it started than I was told. I screamed and cried just like the other girls I had heard while I was waiting before my turn. In about five minutes it was over. Then I was cleaned up and the real pain came, the cramps, which were much worse. I was just in awful pain. Not only did I just lose my fiancé, but I just killed a child. I was given pain meds but didn't want them, I just wanted to leave and recover at home. I never thought I would feel as bad as I did. I was an emotional wreck on top of the physical pain.

The nurse came to check on me and asked if I wanted to know if it was a boy or girl. I said no, I just wanted to go home. I never wanted to give another thought about that baby or the abortion. Another woman came in to give me instructions before I left and smugly said, "Your baby boy is no longer your problem."

How cold! I was overwhelmed by that remark and never forgot it. It haunted me for many years.

I did eventually marry and became pregnant with my first child at 31. As I was looking at some pamphlets in the waiting room of the doctor's office, I saw a pregnancy chart in full color showing all nine months and how the fetus looks as it grows and develops. I quickly focused on the four-month's picture and I started to weep. It didn't look at all like the fetal tissue I was told it was before my abortion, it looked like a child, a real, living baby! Oh my God, I had actually killed a living being—my baby boy never got a choice. I removed him and he never got a chance at life. For the first time, I realized what I had really done and it sickened me. Had I known everything about pregnancy then, I am not so sure I would have made that choice to abort. The grief and feelings of remorse and shame filled my heart.

At age 31, I had another life growing inside of me and I was so glad to have another chance to be a mother. I wanted this baby more than I have ever wanted anything else in my life.

My pregnancy went very well until a few weeks before my due date when the doctor told me the baby hadn't turned, but not to worry. He took an ultrasound and discovered John had a short cord and probably couldn't make it through the birth canal, and if he turned, the cord would wrap around his neck, so I was monitored closely. John was face up and the umbilical cord was wrapped around his neck, so my doctor called for a C-section the next week.

I was checked into Saint John's hospital in Santa Monica, California on May 18 to get ready for an early morning surgery. As I lay there alone, a priest came in. He was speaking in Latin and had incense flowing from a small container. He was pretty old but seemed very interested in me and was saying prayers. I quickly called for the nurse and she came in and told him to leave, that this patient was having a baby and he was in the wrong room. I asked the nurse why was he here, she said he was giving last rites, he thought you were dying. Oh my goodness, now I was nervous at the thought of getting last rites before surgery! Yuck.

The surgery really didn't scare me, I was too excited to meet John and be his mom. I was given two spinal blocks because the first didn't take completely to make me numb. Finally, I was still awake but felt nothing. John came in weighing seven pounds three ounces, and was nineteen inches long. He was screaming and a little blue, and he was put in an incubator. I could see he was okay, and I relaxed as I was stitched up. I wanted to see my baby as soon as possible. I was wheeled into recovery only to see lots of people crying and shaking their heads, looking very concerned. What is going on, is it my baby, is he okay? The nurse replied, he is fine, while you were in surgery, Mount Saint Helens erupted. She placed me in a room with a TV so I could see what was going on. It was awful and there was so much destruction. Wow, that is a birthday John and I will never forget.

As a new mother, I was overwhelmed with many emotions, I wanted to be a good mother but how could I after the mother who raised me caused me to have fearful emotions? I didn't want to ever treat John the way I was treated.

All my life I felt somewhat out of place, not totally accepted and only knowing love at a distance. After I gave birth to John, I knew what a mother's love really meant. When I was recovering from the surgery, I looked at this beautiful life and I was instantly connected to this person I didn't even know. I touched his tiny face, his beautiful lips, his tiny fingers and toes. He was created inside of me, he is my child. It was a connection I never knew could exist. When he cried, I felt something. When he laughed, I felt it again, an emotion deep within my heart and soul. When he went to sleep, I just stared at him. When he woke up, I was there. When he needed love and kisses, I was there. Breastfeeding was a pleasure, a warmth and closeness I can't explain. This was a bond I now know my birth mother had taken away from her.

All children will challenge you, even adopted children, so be ready, it is all worth it. I felt all the same feelings for Daniel, my second child. And then I thought of the child I aborted, how could I have killed such a precious life just because of my own insecurities and fears? All I could do now was be the best mom I could and ask God's forgiveness.

With Daniel, I had a great pregnancy and no problems with his delivery either. Though it too was a C-section, I was prepared. He was just as beautiful to me as John. I knew two children were enough for me so I choose to have my tubes tied to prevent any further pregnancies. I was thirty-three after Daniel was born and I knew raising children was a full time labor of love. For me, two was plenty, and such a blessing.

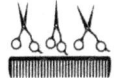

Salon Story

Cat Fight and Rollers Flying

I was working in Florida in a large salon when one of my regular customers was telling me her husband was cheating on her and she had been tracking him using a private eye. Her story was very interesting, but I was afraid what she would do once she had all her proof. While she's telling me the story, another female client was relaxing under the dryer. I proceeded to finish putting rollers in my client's hair and lead her to the dryers. She showed me a picture of the woman her husband was cheating with. I got choked up, I knew this woman. In fact, it was the very same woman who was relaxing under the dryer. Now the wife will be sitting next to her husband's lover. I prayed she didn't put two and two together, but almost right away she saw her and the cat fight began. Rollers were flying and the cursing, yelling, and fighting was at an all-time high for the salon. Several of us stepped in to separate the women and the police were called. We got both of them outside and my rollers were scattered everywhere. Finally the police came and broke up the fight as it continued on the sidewalk and took them both in. I am pretty sure I am still missing some rollers!

The Lockbox, the Cat, and Mom

There was a time in my life that I thought life was too much to bear. I was working in my salon in Carmel, California after moving from Los Angeles with two small children. My husband at that time was not working, so I was the primary breadwinner. I leased two businesses in Carmel and put my husband to work; hoping he could pitch in and help contribute to our income. For a while, it seemed to be going well. I had my kids in daycare, and business was growing. I employed fifteen people, most in the beauty salon while my husband ran a tanning center with three employees. It is very expensive to run two businesses in Carmel as well as maintain rent at a house. I seemed to be working seventeen-hour days. I knew I had to keep pushing to make it all work.

One day I got a call from my mother's bank in North Carolina; it seems she was giving away her money and possessions and was down to one certificate of deposit that was getting ready to be available, and after that, she would be broke. I checked in with a neighbor of hers and discovered it was true. My heroin-addicted brother and his friends had been staying with her, stealing from her, and pawning her possessions. I told my husband he needed to go there and check out the situation, and if necessary, bring Mom to Carmel to live with us. It was not something I wanted to do, but I felt it was the right thing to do.

So he left for Fayetteville and when he got there, things were worse off than we thought. He grabbed Mom's clothes, some personal items and her cat, along with a black, locked box that he thought might contain some legal papers. He loaded the car up to overflowing. He turned in her apartment keys and got her out of her lease. When he called, he said Mother was in worse shape than we had thought, that her memory was bad and she was confused, that she was drinking heavily and her apartment reeked of cat pee and cat food. She looked unkempt and awful. This was a far cry from the mother I remembered who was always well-groomed, wore expensive clothes, and always had her hair coiffed. She epitomized the phrase, "dressed to the nines."

During the drive from North Carolina to California, she smoked, cussed, yelled, and was a real pain in the butt for my husband, and the cat—well he peed and pooped all over the car since Mom wouldn't let him stay in the carrier. It was the trip from hell. I knew we had made a big mistake bringing her to live with us, but I was determined to help her regardless of what I felt.

When they arrived, she was in awful shape. My husband was really upset and he wanted to send her back. I had her examined by a doctor who told me she had early Alzheimer's. Everything ahead was going to be increasingly difficult and those things were explained to me, but I wanted to try to be a good daughter and help her.

That first year did me in. She was mean to me and the children; she cussed at my husband every time he saw her; while I was at work she called the police on me saying I had kidnapped her; she started writing checks out to whoever came to the door; and she wouldn't bathe for days and weeks. Along with her drinking and smoking, I finally had had enough. She was violent and increased her abuse toward us. I was fearful for her and all of us. I contacted a community that specialized in care for Alzheimer's patients, made arrangements for her long-term care in Fayetteville, and put her on a train with an assistant. The airlines wouldn't take her without a family member and I was not going to fly with this violent woman, so she had to travel by train. I loaded her up with all of her personal things—but not that black box.

I was contacted by Amtrak in the wee hours of the next morning to inform me that Mom went missing. The assistant went to the restroom, and when she returned, Mom was gone. I was hopping mad and worried, wondering where was she and how this could possibly happen. It took five hours for Amtrak to locate her. She had switched trains and was now in a train station in downtown Los Angeles. Oh my goodness, only seven hours from Carmel—she hadn't even left the state! I was furious at Amtrak and gave them an earful. By this time, the train she was on had finished its run and was at the LA station for the night.

Amtrak arranged for her and an assistant to get on a bus, one that wasn't stopping. Finally, she reached North Carolina and someone from the care facility was there to pick her up and check her into her new home. After nearly three days, Mom was in a bad way and needed more care. I was told she would be well taken care of, so I trusted that she would be. After one month, I got a call that Mom was being very violent and we discussed medicines and that she was allowed wine with a meal. She insisted on it and they allowed it. I could only agree and asked for a doctor to call me about any further issues. I was paying nine hundred dollars a month out of my pocket for her care; part was paid by Medicare, but I picked up the rest as well as any extras that were needed. The cat went to a neighbor, and the black box? Well, it was put in a storage area and remained there forgotten for years. I really had no time to look into it. Life was crazy enough.

    I visited Mom the next year, and she asked if she knew me. I said yes, I was her daughter. She replied, "Oh, you're the one that ruined my life." As I sat there in her room, she just stared at me for about thirty minutes before she started screaming, "Get out! Get out, I hate you!" I could clearly see I had set her off and she needed to be medicated. I made sure she had the care she needed and then left the next day. I never saw her again.

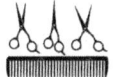

Salon Story

The Rubber Chicken

I owned a huge salon in Carmel, California. Carmel is known for its breathtaking coastline and unique town and beaches. There are all kinds of unique people who pass in and out of this area and some came into my salon.

A couple of traveling women came in one day looking for haircuts, not unusual at all, but when they brought out a rubber chicken and treated it like a third sister, things got weird. They asked if I would take their pictures with it before and after their haircuts and then they placed it in my styling chair and asked me to pose with it as if I was cutting its hair too—oops, I mean feathers, that is. Oh my, I could hardly keep a straight face. They told me they traveled everywhere with this rubber chicken, it was their funny companion. I had seen the movie Sisterhood of the Traveling Pants, but a rubber chicken? Expect the unexpected; you just never know what life will bring your way.

CERTIFICATE OF BIRTH

Registry-Office   S a l z b u r g   Nr 1043/1949
------------ <u>Hermine</u> Anna Matejovic ----------------------
was born on 12 June 1949 at 19 hrs 30 minutes ----------
at Salzburg, 48 Müllner Hauptstrasse --------------------
             Mother: Gertrud Matejovic, assistant worker,
Catholic, residing at Salzburg, 15 Linzerstrasse -------

             Changes of Records:

                          <u>Salzburg, 25th of April 1951</u>

Stamp: For the Registrar:
                               sign.: Berger
Registry-Office
of the Land-Capital
S a l z b u r g

Year of the Search

The first year after Vera's death was difficult. Business was okay but it was hard to manage two leases, and we found out the original lease had been altered and shortened before we took it over from the original owners, so the rent doubled after three years, and not ten like it was originally presented. I had a lawyer look it over and sure enough it was amended, but the lawyer never caught it before signing, so I never knew. We had to sell both businesses and move out.

That is when we moved to North Monterey, California, about thirty minutes north of Carmel, and I opened another salon. Most of my customers were loyal and came. It was very difficult and a huge financial loss, but somehow we managed and also bought a house. Life was getting back on track.

Just after I sold my shop, the Northridge Earthquake of 1989, a 7.0, happened. The earth shook for about two weeks. The news showed major damage to highways and homes and lives torn apart. We lived near the epicenter but not right on the fault, so damage in our area was not too bad. But it scared us all.

After recovering from the earthquake, school resumed. Daniel was ten years old and in the fifth grade. I had never thought of searching for my birth mother, but he asked me questions about our family history that I did not know the answers to. He was working on a school project, the family tree. I told him we could do his dad's family tree and he said, "No, I want to do yours." Oh my goodness, I really had no information about my family other than my adoptive family, and by this time, all of them had died. My childhood was not a good one and I didn't want him to feel badly about my life, so I simply said I was adopted and didn't know anything about my birth mother and that my adoptive parents were dead, so I had no information to share with him.

He looked at me with those beautiful, big eyes and those long lashes and asked, "Why don't you know where you came from? Don't you want to know, Mommy?"

Wow. I never thought anyone would be interested in my life at all. I told Daniel that my adoption happened a long time ago and I really wasn't interested in finding out why I was given up. He said bravely, "Mom, you should know, it could be important."

I told him I would try to find things out, but really, I just wanted to let it go. But Daniel would remind me now and then about me saying I would try to discover my birth story.

We ended up doing Daniel's father's family tree, and it was fun because his grandparents were still living and we interviewed them. Daniel completed his assignment, and shortly after that he came back and asked me if I was looking into my family tree. I said, "Looking for what?" He said, "Your birth mother." Okay, he was really after me, so by 1992 I started searching.

In the back of my mind I had a vague memory of a locked box stuffed in a closet with Vera's things in it. Did I dare to open it? What would I find out? As soon as I found it, I got a hammer and started pounding that lock—I was determined to open that box. At first I was excited, then scared, then back to excited. After an hour of beating the lock, it finally broke. Even as glad as I was to get it open, I was a little scared to see what might be in it. One by one, I read every page of those documents. Words that tore me up and words that only provoked more questions can be powerful.

I was forty-two when I saw my adoption documents for the first time. Those words hit me square between the eyes. I had sinking thoughts such as, "What if Vera was right, what if I was a bad seed, a troubled child that no one wanted?"

The first papers I came across were my birth records, both in German and in English. It was then that I discovered my given name; Hermine Anna Matejovic, born June 12, 1949 at 19 hrs 30 minutes, at Salzburg Mullner hospital. Present were Mother Gertrud Matejovic and an assistant aid worker. Religion: Catholic, residing in Salzburg.

Next, I got to a declaration document that read, "The unmarried mother of a child, born on June 12, 1949 gave irrevocable consent of adoption to adoptive parents Lloyd and

```
                                          Salzburg, 8 Oct 1951
M 4587/49-Schei/W
Matejovic Hermine Anna
    12. 6. 49

              Official Confirmation
The Youth Center of the town Salzburg officially confirms herewith
that the illegitimate Hermine Anna Matejovic, by adoption Hermine
Anna Mc Daniel, born on 12 June 1949, is an Austrian citizen by
birth as the child's mother is a native of the municipality of the
town Salzburg.
                           Youth Center of the town Salzburg
                                  Official Guardianship

                                      Sign.: Scheichl
```

```
COPY                                      Salzburg, 10th March 51

M 4587/49-Schei/W
Re: mj.Matejovic Hermine Anna

                    Declaration

    As unmarried mother of the illegitimate child Hermine Anna
    Matejovic, born on 12 June 1949, I voluntarily give herewith
    my legal and irrevocable consent to an adoption of my child
    by adoptive parents chosen by the Youth Center of the town
    Salzburg.

    I positively give herewith my consent to an adoption by them.


    The Official Guardian:              The Child's mother:
    sign.: Scheichl e.h.                sign: Matejovic Gertrud  e.h.


    F.d.R.d.A.: Kaschl
         Youth Center of the town Salzburg
            Official Guardianship
```

Vera McDonald, a chosen child, and maternal rights entirely in favor of this adoption." It was typed in. My birth mother's name was typed in, not signed by her, but typed and signed by the town council on January 30, 1951. How was this possible? My birth mother never signed this declaration at all. I was just over two years old. I felt so confused and was left with even more questions. Where had I been for two years?

Then I read the Application for Petition for Naturalization for me, signed by Vera and Lloyd McDaniel, along with many military papers and records from the army and the township of Salzburg, Austria. Some papers called them my foster parents and some my adopted parents. Nowhere did I see my birth mother's consent or signature. It was like everyone was making decisions without my birth mother's involvement. More questions grew as I kept searching. Next, there it was in big letters, "unmarried mother of the illegitimate child." That was me! I cried out, me, illegitimate!

All the papers had an official seal and were written in legal form. One paper even said I had been abandoned by my maternal mother. Then a document called Displaced

Person's Act of 1948 appeared in my hands, explaining how a child becomes a ward of the township. There was the official adoption contract, handwritten with Vera and Lloyd McDaniel, and the Municipal Youth Administration office of the Guardian for the township of Salzburg. My birth mother's signature was not on these papers either. All of it was approved through the Tudors court.

```
                        HEADQUARTERS
                UNITED STATES FORCES IN AUSTRIA
                   Office of the Provost Marshal
                        APO 168, US ARMY

                                              29 May 1951

SUBJECT: Request for Permission to Submit to the Jurisdiction of
         an Austrian Court

TO     : Commanding General
         United States Forces in Austria
         APO 168, US Army

    1. Reference: letter, Hq, USFA, AG 008 GAP, 9 December 1950,
subject: "Adoption Proceedings in Austria."

    2. Permission is requested to submit to the jurisdiction of
the Austrian Court in order to adopt a child.

    3. The child, Hermine Anna Matejovic, Austrian citizen, age
one year, eleven months, is presently a ward of the Jugendamt
(Child Welfare), Salzburg, Austria.

    4. The undersigned adopting parents have been married eighteen
years. The adoption of this child is desired due to the physical
inability of the adopting parents to have children of their own.


         Vera M. McDaniel           Lloyd L. McDaniel
         Vera M. McDaniel           Lloyd L. McDaniel
                                    Lt Colonel   MPC

6 Incls:
    1. Birth Certificate of Child (Original Document)
    2. Birth Certificate of Child (Translation)
    3. Certificate - US Legal Officer
    4. Contract of Adoption (Original)
    5. Contract of Adoption (Translation)
    6. Statement - Adopting Parents
```

Then I found my adoptive father's death certificate. Wow, that was a surprise. There was the real cause of his death, a malignant melanoma and a heart attack on April 22, 1972; two days before Vera's birthday. Then I found Dad's will, dated 1955—another surprise. Everything was left to Vera in case of his death; Robbie and I were to inherit what was left after her death. Of course, Vera spent everything or gave it away before she died and wouldn't let me or anyone else have anything. She even gave our housekeeper a diamond bracelet worth eight thousand dollars. Robbie, high on heroin at the time, pawned a lot of silver and collectibles to support his addiction. Vera gave Robbie money and anything else that he asked her for. There was no inheritance remaining when Vera died; she left no will.

This locked, black box was full of interesting documents, and it did reveal a few things, but I was still left with questions I wanted answers to. It appeared that Dad did most of the paperwork. Also in that locked box were two pictures, one of Robbie and one of me at Christmas with our sleds, the first year we came to America from Austria. I have only a few pictures of my childhood, and few of Robbie. Pictures were not so popular in our family.

Well, there it was, everything I wanted to know. But there was still so much that I didn't know. I sat in my room quietly thinking. The word "illegitimate" kept coming up in my mind. Could Vera have been right, was my birth mother a whore who didn't want me and abandoned me? Why was I one year old when I was put into the orphanage? And how did I end up in America with a couple who treated me so badly? And why did I have to bury everyone in my adoptive family? One day I would get the answers I longed for.

And so it began.

First, I located United Adoptees International to find my birth mother, Gertrud Matejovic. This organization helps people search for their birth families and support each other through the often long and difficult process. I got some good advice and found it all very interesting on how to start your search, but they did not do searches outside of the US. So then I needed help searching outside of the US. I had some records, copies, no original documents, but nonetheless, I had a lot of information from that black box to put in the right hands when I found them.

It took another two years till I had my first real lead. A dear customer of mine for several years gave me a name to contact when she learned about my search. It was very hard for her to tell me her story and share her search with me, but as we got to know each other better, she did. Mary had given up her search for her son that she had given up, but then he found her when he turned eighteen years old.

They still keep in touch today. Mary was married to a German resident, and he was controlling and adamant about not having children. When Mary got pregnant, he threatened to kill her and the baby. She gave that baby up at the hospital. A year later, the husband was arrested and she was finally free. Her story and the information that she gave me on finding a searcher in Austria opened a huge door for me.

Mary joined in by writing letters to the Salvation Army and various embassies in Germany and Austria. She looked at all the names on my adoption records and personal mail regarding my birth records. She searched everywhere for those names. Her search turned up little information, but I did follow through on some leads. We found records of the aid worker who cared for me at the orphanage; she had died many years before my search began. The embassies were of

Aid Worker

little help, as their records were tightly sealed. I searched the army records at that time and they were not helpful either.

Leonnie Bomehmer is a searcher from Germany who helps locate people scattered and displaced by the wars. She was just the person I needed. She is a true blessing. I knew I was on my way to meet my birth mother. Daniel was right, I should know the truth, whatever it turned out to be.

The search letters went out to Germany and Austria in 1993. I made contact with Leonnie and she accepted my search request. She only asked in return that I pay for any documents and correspondence that incurred a cost, she never asked for a fee. I was amazed that a total stranger in Germany would take my case for free. I was getting more and more excited at the possibility of someday soon meeting my mother.

My emotions were mixed; will she want to meet me? Will she be honest with me? Why did she give me up and who is my father? Who, what, where, what if—all these questions popped into my head as I got more excited about my search. Since my childhood was full of rejection and feelings of abandonment, I thought, no matter what, I could handle whatever truth—or untruth—turned up. The excitement was building inside of me.

After six weeks Leonnie had an address, location, and phone number for my birth mother. She gave me very good advice on how to proceed. My search had ended. I found what I was looking for after nearly three years of questions and searching. The rest was up to me. It's hard to describe how I really was feeling, excited, scared, and relieved.

I sat quietly looking at my birth mother's name and her phone number as though it held all the secrets I had so longed for. Before meeting her, I discovered that she had married twice and lived in the small farming community of Ostermiething, Austria, about thirty minutes from Salzburg. Her name now was Gertrud Kainer, and she was sixty-two years old. I was nearly forty-five. Now what? Suddenly, in a single moment, I knew more than I had known all my life about my birth mother. I began to ask myself many more questions and started to back out. Luckily, my friends would not let me; they encouraged me and gave me support. I had a German customer who helped me translate our letters.

Next came the momentous phone call, a three-way call with the translator, and for the first time, I heard my mother's voice. I was shaking as if I was standing in a snowstorm naked, yet hot inside with fear of the unknown. I heard, "Hello?" My interpreter responded after I said, "Is this Gertrud Matejovic, and did you give birth on June 12, 1949 to a girl Hermine?"

Dead silence. Then Gertrud said, "Yes, is this Hermine?"

She responded in broken English and German, and then started to cry and said she never thought she would ever hear from me, that she never stopped praying and thought of me every day and celebrated my birthday every year I was gone. She called me her darling daughter. All my fears melted away and, in that moment, I knew I was supposed to meet her. I felt her genuine love, sadness, and nervousness. We spoke for a few minutes and I asked if she would like for me to come there and meet her. She said, "Of course you can come; I will meet with you." She told me she was sorry that I went away and that she did look for me. I told her, "It is okay; we have found each other now."

After we hung up, my friends all gathered in my salon and we all wept and rejoiced. They started planning my trip to Austria right away and delighted in the reunion they had taken part in. I felt so blessed for all the love and support I received.

I remember getting that first letter from her in the mail a couple of weeks after that life-changing phone call. I treasure it still.

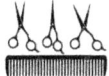

Salon Story

The Stripper

In a salon where I worked in Hollywood, I had a very handsome customer named John, a male stripper and Chippendale dancer. He was also a former boyfriend of Vanna White. John would come in every three weeks, as a model he needed to look good all the time. He was very sweet and he told me he was trying to hide his stripper career from his mother. Unfortunately, a neighbor showed his mother the Playgirl magazine he was featured in and his mother was understandably upset.

He asked me what I would do if my son were a stripper. I told him I would ask him to find a different line of work! But John was a grown man and what he did for work was really not my business. I told him to tell his mom what he did and that it was not meant to hurt or embarrass her; it was just something temporary that paid well. He then proceeded to show me the photos in Playgirl that his mother saw. I started to sweat and felt really embarrassed, and I was still holding scissors! I was trembling slightly but managed to cut his hair.

A few weeks later, I heard he had died while walking near a small plane on the runway about to take off. A strong gust of wind tumbled the plane and killed him. He was dead at twenty-eight. Life is short, you never know when your day comes, so talk well of others, love as much as possible, and never judge anyone but yourself.

When the Train Pulled into the Station

After nearly nine months of phone calls and letters, it was time to board the plane for the long flight to Salzburg. My children and their father took me to the airport in San Francisco, about forty-five minutes from where we lived. As I recall, it was a beautiful day. I traveled late in the day so I could sleep most of the way through the night as it was a very long flight and a seven-hour time change. I had arranged for Gertrud to meet me very early in the morning at a train station in Ostermiething where she lived. The closest airport was in Salzburg was about forty-five minutes away, so I took a commuter train to Ostermiething. The rail system is wonderful there. I didn't speak German, so I asked if anyone riding spoke English, and one man raised his hand. I introduced myself and asked if he would let me know when my stop came so I wouldn't miss getting off. He said of course, he would be glad to help out. I was more than ready and waited for his thumbs up.

It seemed that everyone knew I was from America, or maybe it seemed that way to me because everyone was looking at me fumble around and speak in English. As I found my way into a seat, I noticed many different looking people. The man sitting across from me was dressed in a white robe and sandals with his head wrapped up, similar to people in religious groups. He was alone and within a few minutes, I noticed a very foul order coming from him and where he was sitting. It nearly blocked my breathing. He was also smoking a hookah, but the smoke from that seemed better than his body odor. He was sweating and chanting, it was all very disturbing. I tried not to look at him but I was a bit fascinated by his appearance and some of the things he was doing, like chanting and talking in a foreign language. He was reading from the Koran, and his eyes were glossy, as if he needed to go to sleep but was trying hard to stay awake. This went on for the entire trip of nearly an hour.

The other passengers didn't seem bothered; most of them were dozing off or listening to music through headphones. There were some children scattered about, they were bored and running up and down the aisle yelling and playing. No food was served as it was now early in the morning. The man across from me had some wrapped food he was eating and his luggage was tight up next to him and he never left them unattended. I had put mine in a compartment but most of the passengers kept their luggage with them.

Although an hour isn't a long time, being by yourself in a foreign country, time seemed to stand still. I started writing down my thoughts and questions I wanted to ask Gertrud. As I wrote, I got more and more nervous. Not knowing anything about my adoption and who my birth father was, I guess I made myself more concerned than I should have. I have always been a strong, forward person. If I wanted to know something, I went in headfirst investigating.

For more than nine months, my birth mother and I had stayed in touch through letters, pictures, and phone calls.

From what I could tell from our communication so far, she was very humble, sweet, and just an ordinary simple woman, living in a rural countryside. It is beautiful where she lives, far removed from big cities. It was peaceful and the people there lived a very simple life, not the fast pace we are used to here in America. I thought I had a lot of information from our communications, but nothing prepared me for what my birth mother told me two days before I left Austria.

Back to the train ride. After about fifteen minutes, the conductor announced the first stop and then the next in German. Not knowing what he was saying, I looked for the man who told me he spoke English. I spotted him and gave the thumbs up or down, and he replied with thumbs down. A few more stops were called out. I noticed each stop was very fast, you needed to get your luggage and get ready or you wouldn't make it out before the doors closed. I had a pretty large suitcase and it was difficult for me to lift. I was worried about those doors closing on me. I got my suitcase and like everyone else I put it with me for a fast getaway. Finally my stop came up and the man yelled in English, "Lady, you're next." Wow, I was almost there. I wondered if Gertrud would be there and who would be with her and how would we talk to each other since her English was very limited. I had her picture with me and she had mine.

The train slowed down, my stop was called out, and I had seconds to get out with my luggage. To my surprise, the smelly man across from me stood up and helped me get my suitcase out. He moved very quickly, and it startled me. I guess you don't have to speak another language to get help; it was obvious I needed it. I felt sad that I had such strange thoughts about him when he turned out to be so polite and helpful.

I got out on the walkway with my luggage and saw Gertrud and two other people—Johann, her husband and her personal nurse who also served as her interpreter—approaching me. They were smiling and walking rather fast. One lady yelled out in broken English, "Marsha, is that you?" I looked up and said yes.

Gertrud came up to me very close, looking at me, and I hugged her to let her know it was all going to be okay. At first I thought she was afraid to hug me, but after I took the lead, she and Johann and the other woman surrounded me and hugged me for about five minutes, saying nothing at all. The woman with Gertrud was her nurse and friend; she had been interpreting my letters for Gertrud. She was in her forties, married with grown children and very sweet. Gertrud and Johann didn't drive when it was dark and they needed her to help interpret. She often became our bridge over troubled communication waters. I am sure the nurse didn't know much about Gertrud's past before I came into her life.

I turned forty-five during my stay in Austria; I was two and a half when Gertrud last saw me. Forty-three years had come and gone. As we walked arm and arm to the car, she was trying to speak and started to cry with joy and fear. The fear was answering my questions--and I was full of questions--but for now I just allowed the emotional moment to settle in. She stared at me and held my hands, saying over and over, "My darling daughter, you are really here, I have always loved you, you are so beautiful." Tears filled her eyes and mine; it was overwhelming at times. I never knew her, yet I felt loved and closer to her than I had ever thought I could have felt.

As we drove to her house, she told me they had paid for me to stay at an inn two blocks from their house and Johann would pick me up every day and make breakfast for us. We drove by her small cottage house, and then to the inn nearby. We were all getting emotionally and physically tired. The time difference really made me very tired and I get chatty when I haven't slept, plus the language difference was extremely difficult for us all. Johann checked me in and made sure I had a good clean room and felt safe. He had already paid for my two-week stay from the money they had saved. I locked the door and as I did, Johann struggled to tell me he would be back later to pick me up for lunch—always speaking in German with large hand gestures. I wasn't sure what time breakfast or lunch was served. I gave him a hug and he left at about 8:30 a.m.

As glad as I was to be there, I was very nervous about the two weeks ahead of me. The electricity was different, and the toilet and the shower took a bit of getting used to. The water seemed softer than ours; the shower was just a handheld wand and had very poor pressure. I did buy an adapter for my curling iron and blow dryer, but when I started using the blow dryer, it got very hot very fast and I had to get my hair dry faster than usual. I never thought my hair looked very good, but no one seemed to notice.

It was summertime, June, so the temperature was warm but not hot. I found it to be really nice and the countryside breathtakingly beautiful. I slept about four hours. Apparently Johann had come earlier but I didn't hear him. I woke up about 12:30 p.m. Austrian time. Johann came back again just as I was stepping out of the bathroom, and I told him to wait, that I would be ready soon. I tried to talk slowly and clearly, but he just answered me in German. I kept talking and he waited about ten minutes outside of the room till I was dressed and ready for him to come in. I asked him to sit, I would be ready very soon and he seemed to understand that I needed to put on makeup and fix my hair. It was like playing charades with him.

Johann is a very simple man with a weathered face and a big smile. He is about five foot ten inches with a very slender build. He was a retired construction worker, a really harsh and physical job where he worked in all kinds of weather. The labor was much harder than in the US because they did not have access to all the heavy equipment we have here. His hands had calluses and lots of cracks. His face showed his weather-beaten character. He was a hardworking, proud man who wanted to provide for Gertrud. He owned an old Jeep, which is what he drove me around in. Of course the area was very rural with no big highways like ours in the States. There were not many road signs or markings, and a lot of hills with narrow roads and even some dirt roads.

Johann greeted me each morning and came to escort me to breakfast at their house. He is a very sweet man, but he couldn't speak a lick of English. Funny how the language of love and affection doesn't require words, we managed with hand signals.

There was a fresh meat market at every corner as well as fresh produce stands. It was wonderful to see people shopping fresh every day. Most people did not have good refrigeration, so that was one reason for shopping daily. The more I stayed with them, the more I saw firsthand how simple their life really was. The nurse came over after lunch to take us out to her house for dinner later that night. Austrians eat a bigger meal at lunch and a light meal at dinner.

She lived in a more modern area than Gertrud, about a twenty-minute drive from there. Her house was larger and on a hill with a beautiful view and many modern amenities that Gertrud didn't have. I saw how humble and how poor Gertrud really was, but at the same time, so content. I saw how much she and Johann loved and took care of each other and how doing little things brought them much joy. We all sat outside drinking wine and eating appetizers and just enjoying small talk. Johann said very little but the nurse interpreted for him and Gertrud. She seemed very concerned about Gertrud. I found out that if you were an outpatient from a hospital in Austria, you were sent a regular nurse once a week for life. Gertrud had been in and out of hospitals for a few years and this nurse was a kind companion.

Gertrud had a hysterectomy, vein surgery, pneumonia, serious bladder issues, and other things she never discussed with me—it was hard to get the real stories.

The nurse was so kind and loving toward all of us. She made sure I sat next to Gertrud and that I was comfortable and well fed. After dinner the nurse started to ask Gertrud how she felt to have me there, was she sleeping okay, and was she taking her medication every day? I had to ask for interpretations and at one point, the nurse didn't reply, just smiled at me. I asked her if Gertrud's health was more serious than she let on. She said she had had her share of bad times but did not really answer me directly. Gertrud was always staring at me, smiling and holding my hand every time we were together. Johann would always walk me back to the inn and wait till I was in the room and locked the door.

They went to bed very early, around 8 p.m., and for the first week, I was still on the wrong time zone and not ready to go to bed. After he left, I walked outside just to sit and think. I got a glass of wine and a notebook and just enjoyed being with my thoughts. At 10 p.m. Austria time, I finally turned in. The jet lag was finally getting to me.

After the first week of touring Ostermiething, I rented a car. I wanted to go into Salzburg but Johann didn't drive the

Autobahn, the traffic was awful and very fast. I wasn't sure I wanted to drive it either but I needed to get to Salzburg to see the "big books" in an old courthouse district in Salzburg near Mirabell Plaza. This place was huge. I took Gertrud and Johann with me; she wanted to show me around. This place held all the records of everyone ever born or who lived in Salzburg, dating back before WWI. These were recordings in very large books, all handwritten. I was allowed to look but not to have copies. I wanted to take a picture but that was not allowed either. We were led into a huge library of books with shelving from floor to ceiling, rows and rows. It was overwhelming to me. Gertrud showed her ID and my date of birth, and the search began.

After about ten minutes, a big book was brought down and there was my name, Gertrud's, the hospital, and the date and time of my birth; just like my copies, but these were the original documents. I don't know how I ever got copies of anything because they were opposed to any recordings ever leaving that building, but I did have them and all the information matched up probably because the military required them to.

It was then that Gertrud asked about a boy baby she had, Wolfgang. This was the first time I heard anything about a half-brother. We looked at his records too. He was adopted out as a baby, only one day old to a military couple. He was three and a half years younger than I was, so I was already gone by the time he was born. Gertrud began to weep silently; I could see clearly how painful this was for her. I am sure she wanted to keep the past hidden in her heart. I, however, wanted all the information I could find. After all, I only had one more week left to get all the answers to the questions that she was avoiding.

Visit to Salzburg

We visited amazing castles, historical sites, and many gardens while we were there. This was when I found out how impatient Johann really is. He wanted to go home, and he started yelling about us leaving. He was not interested in me driving or walking around anymore and told Gertrud he would get a cab, and he walked off and left us.

Wow, that was awkward. She told me not to give it any thought, Johann didn't like leaving Ostermiething, he would be home waiting for us (which he was with prepared snacks, seeming totally okay, as if nothing happened). Her broken English took a long time for me to understand but I knew some words she was trying to say and we managed just fine.

I have to say I was very nervous about driving in Salzburg. There are traffic circles and narrow one-ways plus we drove on the opposite side of the road. I didn't know the driving laws and there were no traffic signs; you just kept up with the flow. I was in a VW Jetta and most people drive a stick shift, but I had to have an automatic.

After an all-day outing we left the beautiful, scenic castles of Salzburg. We had shopped and saw where the *Sound of Music* was filmed and walked the historic town where Mozart lived and created the beautiful music he left behind.

The Danube River could be clearly seen as well as the massive churches, which were amazing. We went into coffee houses and shops along the way; it was a time I will never forget. The pictures and travel brochures didn't show the full beauty as being there did. There was one castle owned and built by an eccentric king, it was called The Castle of Trick Fountains. There were squirts of water that would go off all over, there was a table with trick fountains built in and when the king wanted his guests to go home, he set them off. We also visited an amazing puppet theater, all of them handmade, which was whimsical and wonderful. The churches are very ornate and had huge domes. The architecture was really beautiful as well as the history. I would love to visit again one day.

As my two weeks started winding down, I still had not gotten answers to all my questions; it seemed Gertrud had a harder time with facing truths than I did. I asked her about how I was born and who my father was and why was I put in an orphanage, questions she struggled to give a straight answer to. I was more than ready, but she wasn't. I wanted to know if my father was alive and who my relatives were and where they all are now.

She told me two days before I had to leave that she wanted to take me somewhere to show me something and she would try to answer my questions. We took a drive, just her and me; we went to a rundown part of the outskirts of the city, an area with abandoned buildings.

As she pointed to a large building, she said, "That's where I worked." I asked what kind of place it was and she said, "a hotel." Okay, so she worked in a hotel.

She proceeded to tell me, "I was a prostitute there on and off for many years after you were taken away."

That is where she met both of her husbands. She started telling me the story of how her first husband died in her arms after a fatal fall on a barge they both owned and worked on, and how Johann, her second husband, rescued her from prostitution. She wept silently, with heavy breathing. I listened intently, and let her go on. She said that was all after I was taken and that it continued after she had had Wolfgang, and she asked me to find him. She then asked me to take her home and I did. She wanted Johann to be there when she told me the rest. This was two days before I was to leave Austria.

We all sat down after dinner that night looking at each other, Johann holding her hands, telling her it was okay, that he would never leave her and I needed to know. "Go on. Tell her, she has a right to know now," he said sternly.

"You want to know who your father was?"

"Yes," I said.

She struggled to talk, so I asked, "Is he dead? Did you know him well? Who is my father?"

She said, "Yes, I knew your father very well, and yes, he is dead."

She sat quietly crying, and then she said, "I was young, only sixteen when we met, he was older and married. He was my first love. He was so excited that I was pregnant with you because he'd never been a father. By the time I was seventeen, you were born, and my lover soon had to leave, but he didn't want to go without you, so he promised if I would put you in an orphanage, he would arrange for us both to go to America. He would get papers for me to be a housekeeper and take care of us both. He was handsome and a lieutenant in the army. He was called Mac by his buddies and that is what I called him. But I did not go to America with him. After eighteen months he, his wife, you, and another child left Austria without me. I didn't know where you went, and I never gave my permission for you to be taken from me. I visited you at the orphanage every week."

I was stunned. This was not the answer I thought I would receive. I said, "Do you mean that Mac, my adoptive father is actually my birth father and he never told me? He was your lover?" It was too hard to fully understand and my mouth hung open in shock. And like a flash of lightning, everything became clear.

"Yes, my darling daughter," she said. "Your real father adopted and raised you. I am so sorry I could not do anything. I tried but it was too late. I was so young without any money or resources to get help. The army was closed-mouthed about it all."

"So I was legally kidnapped?" I asked her. "Taken without your permission?"

"Yes," she said.

She knew before I came to Austria that Mac was dead. I had told her in a letter about both parents being dead. No wonder it was so hard for her to tell me. She knew things only someone intimate could know, such as his habits, his nickname, his rank, and the timeframe during which he lived in Austria. She even had a photo of him. There was no denying the truth.

We sat and held each other, crying silent tears of familiar pain and sorrow. I was sad for her and the life she had led and I was sad that I never knew the truth about my father. I also now knew the real reason Vera treated me so badly. I was a constant reminder of her husband's infidelity. She raised a child that he had with someone else and then was forced to lie to everyone about it for a lifetime.

The disturbing truth didn't sink in till I got home and I thought about how he denied my birth on all the records and my citizenship. The depth of lies and a lifetime of cover-ups made me angry and sad at the same time. My entire childhood was a lie. A million thoughts were racing through my mind. Knowing that I was the child of an affair was bad enough, but being a child stolen from her mother and home country, and denied my birthright was hard to bear. Normally, when you are born to an American outside the United States, you are granted dual citizenship. In my case, the Austrian citizenship was recorded, but left there when I was brought to America. It was as though I was never Austrian at all. I became an American citizen through adoption, but really, I was born to an American father.

I told Gertrud before I left that I was glad I came and met her and glad she told me the truth because it really did help us both cope with a disturbing past. As difficult as it was, truth is always better than a lie. If you can handle the truth, you will be okay.

I am grateful I knew my father, even through the lies. My father was dead, Vera was dead, and my brother was dead. There was no one to ask questions of anymore. I was left with only the lies they told me over a lifetime. I had to leave the next day, so I spent the night pulling myself together in order to face Gertrud and be able to spend my last day with her on a happier note. I had a quiet day with Gertrud and Johann taking walks, talking, eating, and enjoying the beautiful countryside. We shared just enough English to communicate. Even so, it was a difficult day. I now possessed all the information I had yearned for. I met my birth mother and got to know how I became adopted and lived in an orphanage till I was two and a half. All my questions were answered, the truth was revealed and now I had to choose how to process it all. Because my father chose to have an affair and lie about it, I grew up abused and neglected by both of my parents—was that fair? What would have happened if Dad had told the truth? Would he have lived longer, would I have understood, would Vera have stayed married to him if he were completely honest with me? How would my life have been different if I had known the truth from the start? I will never know, and have come to accept this fact.

I knew I had to forgive those who had hurt me and I had to deal with years of lies. It has not been easy, but necessary. If I had one more day with my dad, I would ask him why he took such a risk. He would probably say he loved me enough to not leave Austria without me, no matter how hard it was. He would probably also tell me that he found himself loving two women and stuck in a situation he couldn't change. I am not sure I could raise a love child, a child born outside of my marriage; I hope I never have to.

I chose to forgive Dad and Vera. I no longer hold anything against anyone and I am glad to have the truth and a good life despite my upbringing. Just because bad things happen to you in life doesn't mean that you have to live a bad life. Seek truth, seek forgiveness. Seek your value and your worth and do not believe the lies people may tell you about yourself. Seek people who are like-minded and can lift you up and honor who you have become.

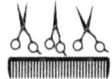

Salon Story

Wigging Out in Beverly Hills

In Beverly Hills I worked for Elizabeth Arden on Rodeo Drive. I was really excited to be in such a high-end salon with celebrities. I was asked to do the hair on four mannequins in the window. Of course I thought it would be a great way to showcase my work, but I found out the window was not very deep and there was not much room to get around the mannequins. I was ready to take their heads off to make it easier to style the wigs but was told I couldn't. It was a very tight area and I got very hot in there with my girls. It took me a long time but I did get them done and they looked great. They each wore a Bob Mackie dress worth thousands!

I thought for sure my name would be in lights, but sadly I was just one of many stylists doing my job, no fanfare or rewards, just a job well done. That was the only time I was ever asked to do mannequins. Not because I didn't do a good job, it was just that these mannequins were never used again. The four mannequins were exquisitely beautiful and detailed and I enjoyed looking at them every day till they left, never to return. I should have had my picture taken with them.

ONE YEAR LATER

One year after meeting Gertrud, I got my last letter from her, a letter of much sadness, telling me she had to move into a hospital care place because of Parkinson's disease. Not only would she be no longer able to take care of herself, but with her shakes, she could no longer write to me either. She told me not to try to find her, just remember our visit. She also said how much she loved me and how glad she was that I knew the truth and forgave her. She wanted me to remember our time together and not to worry or be sad for her. I wrote her back and the letter was returned, as were several other letters I wrote. After that, sadly, I had to respect her wishes and there were no more letters. I only have pictures, the truth, and memories to hold on to. I knew my dad after all, and that was important to me.

I cherish our two weeks together and have no regrets about finding her. I explained the story to my sons, and now as adults they understand how special my life

really is and how things aren't always how they appear to be. After the death of both of my parents, Robbie, and numerous other family members, I have learned how important those closest to you really are and every day is a gift I get to unwrap.

It was unfortunate that Dad died so young, at only sixty-two years old. He never got to see me marry or experience the birth of my sons, his grandchildren. Before Robbie died, he did marry and had a little girl, Kimberly, but Dad never met her either. I saw Robbie struggle in torment about his own identity and addiction. He was kind and gentle, but was never at peace with himself. Sadly, another by-product of many adoptions that left people feeling unworthy.

I have been asked many times if I love my birth mother. I have given this a lot of thought and I guess I can say in a way I do, but not the kind of deep, abiding love I wish I could have had if I had lived with her. My love for her comes from knowing the kind of person she is, knowing her kind and gentle manner, her compassion for all living things, her love of God and faith, and her courage to survive under the worst of times, never giving up. My love for her is respectful and trusting. I know she suffered from losing two children in her life and I know she has joy in knowing me and seeing pictures of her only grandchildren. She is at peace now, and so am I. I wish I could be with her one more time. I will never know if she passed away because I don't know where she went. I pray for her daily and for Johann too. I have tried to find him as well. He must have moved too.

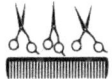

Salon Story

The Decorator

I bought a house high up on a canyon in North Monterrey, California. It was a four bedroom, three-bath home on two acres. I didn't have enough money to decorate with but I knew in time I would. One of my clients was an interior decorator; Joy asked me if I needed anything. I said of course, I needed all kinds of things, so she invited me to her storage locker to choose whatever I wanted from her selection of furniture and accessories. She had some amazing things; after all, she has decorated some of the most elite homes in Pebble Beach. She told me to take whatever I needed and she would have it delivered. She had rich taste and I was just in an average home, how would her stuff blend in with mine? I soon learned that a few very nice pieces blend in with almost anything. I was amazed at how great it looked when I got some nice pieces in the house. Elegant mirrors, wall décor, pillows, pictures, a bedspread, and lots of curtains, foot stools, a sectional sofa, and many more things that I really enjoyed. Thank you, Joy!

Daddy Dearest

My father was an amazing man and husband. If you were to look at his accomplishments in life, you'd be impressed. He graduated college with honors; served thirty-two years in the military; retired as a full-bird colonel; and served as a city manager for our town of Fayetteville, North Carolina as well as Provost Marshal at Fort Bragg during his remaining years in service to the United States Army. Dad served actively in two wars, Korea and Vietnam, and was part of the reconstruction of Europe after WWII. Dad was an excellent paratrooper—a role model for every young man coming up the ranks in the army. He served in the local church and was well respected for his service in the Lions Club for many years. He took very good care of his wife, Vera, whom he loved dearly, and told her so often.

Dad joined the army on April 16, 1933 and met Vera shortly thereafter on his first assignment. For the next eighteen years, they traveled all over the world answering the call and duties of the army, where he eventually became a decorated officer.

Vera was a devoted wife who was actively involved in many service-based clubs, including the March of Dimes. She attended many events supporting her husband and she loved the life he made for them. For eighteen years before they adopted children, life was a dream come true for Vera. When Dad was away for many long weeks and months, she kept them close by writing often and visiting when she could. She took good care of his heart. Vera was also very intelligent. As a college graduate, she had good business skills and took care of running the household, including serving as our disciplinarian, but Dad was the one with the final say about money matters. As was typical of the 1940s and 1950s, he was head of the household.

When Dad was about thirty-seven, he was stationed in Vienna and Salzburg, as part of the American restoration of Europe after the devastation of a thirteen-year war that took the lives of over ten million people. World War II left hundreds of thousands of children, women, and fractured families displaced and living without hope. Troops were stationed in Salzburg from 1944 to 1955, helping put together a strong infrastructure for the people to have a better life and put the war behind them. Most Austrians were left poor, without even some of the most basic items of life they needed; things like radios, washing machines, and other working appliances. The army brought provisions and new technology to the area and spent money to help build up the local economy, put people back to work, and aid those who were displaced and living in refugee or displaced persons (DP) camps and orphanages.

Many widows and younger women were looking for a way out of poverty, a way to flee the desperation and come to America. To accomplish this, they sought to marry American soldiers. The desire for companionship by both the men who were stationed there and the women who sought a way out became a way of life. Regulations were put in place to discourage the soldiers from fraternizing with the women. Dad was an officer leading the platoons that served Vienna and Salzburg. This would become Dad's longest tour of duty, about three and a half years. Early on, Vera wrote and sent packages as she had always done when Dad was deployed, and she requested a hardship pass to go to Austria. After two years, she received a visa to move to Vienna to be with Dad.

They lived in officer housing. When Dad's time in Austria was winding down, they made plans to return to America and move on to Dad's next assignment in Virginia. Vera, with a serving heart, had heard of the many children without parents and had become a rigorously trained volunteer, a "Gray Lady"—wearing the Red Cross gray service uniform—rendering non-medical service and recreational activities to those in need. She served many children who were in dire need of parents and a stable life.

Lloyd and Vera were both nearly forty and were never able to conceive any children of their own, so they talked about adopting. I think Dad was more interested in having children than Vera, but Vera had been visiting a German baby that was in an orphanage in Vienna and he had taken a liking to her. His name was Robert, born in January 1950, and removed from abusive parents at the age of one and a half years old. Vera would call him Robbie and sing songs to him, hold him, and visit often. She made sure Robbie was taken care of, even though he didn't talk or bond well with anyone, he did respond to her. Vera asked Dad if he would meet Robbie and consider adopting him. Dad was a very compassionate man and when he met the child, he saw the joy Robbie brought Vera and the way he responded he to her. Since Vera had already agreed to adopt his daughter, Robbie would help Vera to deal with Dad's love child.

Dad eventually took Vera to meet her. I was nearly two and Dad told Vera all about his affair and how had no idea he could father a child, but he did. In those days, it was considered unlawful for an unwed teenager to keep her child.

Robbie was not in the same orphanage; he was with the Catholic youth housing in Vienna and had become a ward of the country of Austria. Hermine was born in Salzburg in 1949 and was a ward of the youth authority of Salzburg in a state-owned orphanage. This is where displaced persons, especially babies, were taken. Mothers could visit, but most gave up their rights to these babies. But Gertrud never did. This is where the lies began.

Dad checked into the adoption procedures and filed mountains of paperwork. There was a waiting time of six months once you filed to adopt a child. After you are preliminarily approved, you are considered foster parents. During these six months, legal papers are drawn up with both the township of the courts in Austria and the army judges and counsel. Among the necessary papers and approvals were naturalization papers, citizenship adoption applications and, if at all possible, signed permission from the birth parent permanently relinquishing parental rights. But Gertrud never did. It was a long time of specific preparation, but Vera and Dad joyfully endured the process to give Robbie and me a home and become a family.

Finally arriving in the US with two babies, Dad seemed to be happy, but Vera would have been happy with only the one child, Robbie. She lit up when she was with him. Dad made a fuss over me and tried to get Vera to feel the same joy with me as she did with Robbie, but it was never to be. All Vera wanted was to pour her love and affection into Robbie. Robbie needed a lot of love; he was mostly a loner, never played with other children, mostly sat in his crib and rocked back and forth, the repercussions of what we know now to be a response to failure to thrive syndrome. He was late in talking too. He was much larger than most of the other boys his age, and seemed to not show much emotion, neither sadness nor joy. But Vera was determined to break through and give him a life filled with her love, acceptance, and joy. He was a bed wetter and he was nearly four before that stopped. But there were no consequences for him. If I wet the bed, I was punished harshly, so I became a quick learner.

Because we moved so much, it was difficult for us to make friends or feel grounded; Robbie and I both asked lots of questions of our parents. I was the one who asked, "Why this" and "Why that" all the time and if I didn't get the answer I wanted or liked, I kept asking till Mom said, "That's enough." My whole life was full of questions. You could say that even to this day, I am a very curious woman. I remember asking Mom why I was adopted and why I had to leave the orphanage. She always told me that my real mother was a whore and I was her mistake; that she could not care for me and abandoned me at the orphanage. Vera would go on to say that if it wasn't for her, I would still be in that dirty, filthy place, and grow up to be a whore too. She told me I should be grateful that I was adopted and to never forget how lucky I was. I never felt lucky, in fact, I felt unlucky.

When I asked my dad why was I adopted, he would simply say, "Because we wanted you, and you are a perfect fit in this family." Really? I didn't feel like I fit at all. Vera would constantly point out negative things about me and I was always in trouble with her. Spanking and other punishments became a part of my daily life. Lucky, no, I did not feel lucky at all.

With no close friends at school and feeling rejected at home, I started to make up a better life by telling people stories about being adopted and saved from a bad situation.

It was a form of self-protection for me. I thought if I could get people to feel sorry for me, then they would be nice to me or even want to be with me and get to know me. Sometimes people would tell Vera about my stories and she would tell them I was just a liar and couldn't be trusted to tell the truth. Every time one of my false stories came back to her, I got a whipping! You would think I would learn, but I didn't want to tell people what Vera told me, that I was a mistake and my birth mother was a whore, and I was rescued from a filthy orphanage. Yuck, that sounded too hard for me to believe.

Dad was too busy running the army base as the Provost Marshal to be concerned with all of this, so he just said nothing to me at all. I would tell him that Mom whipped me for no good reason. He never believed my pain and sadness were worth a remedy. Vera started telling Dad how hard it was to discipline me and that I needed more of a heavy hand, that he needed to do the whipping sometimes.

That's when Dad really changed; when I was about eight years old. He backed off being nice and listening to me and calling me over to sit by him. He got colder and punished me harshly when Vera reported to him. Vera was always right in Dad's eyes. Her wishes took precedence over my needs or the truth.

The whippings got worse, and once he beat me so badly with a thick, heavy belt that Mom and Robbie had to pull him off me. The buckle on the belt caught my skin and left terrible welts and cuts. I didn't go to school the next day, my butt and legs were too cut and sore to walk. I was about eight at that time and our housekeeper, Marie, came in to work, saw my condition and attended to my wounds. Since we moved so often, I didn't feel I could tell anyone trustworthy how bad it was at home. Vera had already warned my teachers that I was a liar and a storyteller and not to believe anything I said. Every time I reported the whippings to someone out of sheer desperation, Vera would only make it worse for me when I got home. As I got older, I just accepted the fact that I was damaged and unlovable, though I wished in my heart that one day someone would listen, believe me, and really care to help. That day came when I was about ten years old.

My Auntie Lyn came for a visit. She was married to my dad's brother. Lyn and her husband lived in Florida and we seldom ever went to see them. Lyn knew the truth; she heard the wild stories and she would come into my bedroom and hold me as I cried. She told me she cared and loved me and she said she was sorry that my life was so hard, but that one day I would be old enough to be on my own and then I could be free. My memories of my auntie are all precious; she really understood and believed me. She was the only one who stood up for me. After her visits, Dad would tell me that he was sorry he had to be so hard on me, that he just wanted me to learn how to be strong and independent and he wanted me to be good so he wouldn't have to whip me.

Aunt Lyn, her brother & her parents

Dad never yelled at me, he just took part in the whippings, though he never asked me what my side of the story was. He just listened to Vera who would tell him that I was a bad seed and always causing trouble, that I was a liar, and I was disrespectful toward her. In our house, we never answered our parents without calling them Sir or Ma'am. We were taught respect and the proper way to address adults. If we failed, we would get a whipping. Robbie got a mild whack once in a while, but it was really me she was after. She seemed to hate me, to punish me for just existing, but I didn't understand why.

Dad's father, George, came to live with us when I was about twelve and Mom's mother came a year later. With other adults in the house, things started to cool down; Vera was still after me, but not as often. Grandpa would stomp his cane at her and say, "That's enough, Vera!"

Grandpa was an interesting man. He was short on words, but you listened when he spoke. He was frail, nearly eighty, and a creature of habit. I would watch him do the same things in the same way every day. He got more junk mail than I've ever seen and he ordered stuff all the time through the mail. Every day he walked up and down the street and all the neighbors got to know George. He would pet the cats with his cane and use it to stomp on your toes if you got rude. He demanded respect, just like my father did. However, in his later years, after Dad died, Grandpa became more eccentric. Wearing only a raincoat, he took his walks and flashed the neighbors. This drew considerable attention and concern from friends and family alike. Eventually, he was put in a care facility and received necessary medical treatment and restraint. George was only there three months before he died at age eighty-six.

Grandma, Vera's mother, was always kind of crazy. We didn't have a name for it then, but I guess it would be what we call Alzheimer's disease now. She wore a damp washcloth on her head, smoked one cigarette after another, sat at the same corner table in the family room and talked to herself for hours every day. She wouldn't bathe on her own. Our housekeeper had to shower Grandma. She walked around in a daze, getting lost in every room. Grandpa McDaniel was annoyed with her most of the time. Grandma was very frail, probably ninety pounds soaking wet. I don't have any memories of her before she came to live with us or Grandpa either. Grandma was about one or two years younger than Grandpa George.

Dad retired the year I turned sixteen. He became the city manager in the town of Fayetteville where we built a home for their retirement years. By then I was in high school with Robbie. I found school very hard. Scholastically, I struggled to concentrate in class, do the work, and pass the tests. I also felt out of place socially. I didn't seem to fit in anywhere. Vera didn't miss a beat telling me how stupid I was or that if I didn't pass school, I would be a failure the rest of my life. Yet neither Dad nor Vera went out of their way to help me. So I fulfilled Vera's prophecy of being a failure in high school and other areas of my life, only I went several steps further; I dropped out of school in the twelfth grade and sought a career as a hairdresser. Much later, as an adult, I was proud to receive my GED at fifty-three years of age.

Yep, I went to beauty school and aced it. I wanted a career and I wanted to be the best hairdresser I could be. By the time I had my first job at eighteen, I was moving out on my own. I couldn't wait to get out and Vera was happy to make that happen. Dad paid for three months of rent on my apartment, helped me get a car and bought me a set of luggage for my eighteenth birthday. Everyone helped me move out; it was the most support I have ever felt! I never asked my parents for help again.

I stopped by their house for visits and noticed that Grandpa was not doing well; Grandma had died the year before. I would meet my dad for lunch once in a while; it was nice, just the two of us. When I was at the house eating dinner and enjoying my adulthood, there was no more fighting; it seemed to have stopped when I moved out. I didn't like to stay long as Vera was still a bit mean to me and tried to start arguments, and I didn't want to fight with her. Robbie was still at home, but was by then addicted to heroin, and we didn't see much of him unless he needed money.

One night in April 1972 after a dinner at the house with my parents, Dad fell in the family room gasping for breath. An ambulance was called and he was taken to the emergency room, suffering from a heart attack. He was treated at the hospital and resting so I went to visit him. When I arrived at the hospital, the staff told me I was not allowed in to see him. I told them I was his daughter, but Vera had instructed the staff and doctors to not allow me to see him. I was refused all calls and visits; it really hurt me and I thought, "What if he dies and I never get to say goodbye?" I was so insistent on seeing my father that Vera had the army move him from Fayetteville, North Carolina to the Portsmouth Naval Hospital in Arlington, Virginia by a medical helicopter. Why was Vera being so hateful?

I never got to see Dad after he was taken from our home by ambulance. Vera must have been concerned that he would share the secret of my adoption with me as a sort of deathbed confession.

Not knowing he was taken from our local hospital, I called there to find out how he was doing—surely his daughter had a right to at least have an update on her father's condition. I asked if my mother was there and all I got was a very rude nurse telling me she couldn't give out any information to me.

Vera became increasingly difficult to speak with after Dad went into the hospital. Her dislike for me was evident for all to see and she reserved the most personal and punishing words for me. She forbade me from seeing him because she claimed that I was the cause of Dad's stress and resulting heart attack. I was devastated at how much more cruel she had become. I soon discovered the new location where my dad was taken and I called the hospital in Virginia. A very nice nurse told me he had passed away peacefully during the night. I was devastated. It was April 22, 1972.

I could not understand why I was adopted by people who could be so cruel and unloving. I cried bitterly for the days leading up to his funeral. Dad and I were just beginning to build a new relationship as adults—he was more relaxed with me once he was no longer responsible for my care and training in the home—when suddenly, he was gone and all hopes of a future relationship died with him.

The funeral was a big military and city official event in our little town of Fayetteville. Dad was a public figure, as demonstrated by his high rank and stellar career as city manager. Officials closed the city offices for the afternoon, most other businesses had little choice but to stop work for a few hours as traffic clogged the city streets for miles. American flags throughout the area flew at half-staff, and people from everywhere came to our little Methodist church to honor the memory of Retired Lieutenant Colonel Lloyd L. McDaniel.

My dad was only sixty-two years old when he died. After an autopsy, melanoma cancer was found to be the cause of his death. A burial in Arlington National Cemetery was offered, and as a highly decorated officer, he would have every right and honor to be buried there, but Vera had him flown back for a burial and service in Fayetteville. The streets were closed during the funeral procession as he was laid to rest with full military honors and a rose garden was dedicated to him in Cross Creek Cemetery. Formal army uniformed guards, the mayor, city officials, and many hundreds of other well-wishers came to his funeral. A twenty-one gun salute topped off the event with great fanfare, along with the tradition of folding the American flag and presenting it the widow, Vera.

I was beyond grieved, angry, and deeply hurt. Vera didn't say a word to me, she just held on to her dear Robbie who by this time was a full blown heroin addict. He looked like the walking dead. Everyone knew about his drug abuse and was actively concerned, yet Vera only saw her little boy, and she covered for him, never denying him a place to lay his head. It made me sick. I wanted to tell Dad so many things in those last two weeks, but I never got the chance, thanks to Vera. She sold the family home and moved to a townhouse, all while Robbie bled her dry for drug money, to the point where his friends came over to her house to steal her possessions and eat. They even poisoned her cats.

After Dad's death, I moved to California, got married and removed myself from them all. I gave birth to two sons, John and Daniel. I was determined that my love was much different from what I grew up with. I wanted my boys to know I loved them and they were a treasure to me. I taught them about life and consequences without whipping or beating them. I found myself enjoying everything about them and loved being their mother. Their births changed my heart! I guess being adopted meant that love was different for me than for the children raised by their biological parents.

I never experienced the love from my parents that I enjoyed with my own children. I wondered if it was even possible. I had times of great challenges, but through all things I loved them.

After everything I learned, the truth was better than a lie or deception, and love outlasts any problem you ever have. Love will still live on, but anger, hate, and resentment have to die.

My only wish is that my daddy was still here for me to talk to, for him to see what a wonderful person I have become and how my strong will to survive the odds against me turned out. If your faith is strong and your vision isn't blurred, and you know yourself and your Creator, you can make it. My dad and I shared a lot of good memories and a lot of painful ones, I want to remember my father as my teacher and as a great person who did a lot of wonderful things, a loyal man committed to making things right, a man of character and strength, an honest and strong man who became respected in his career, who loved his country and served it well, a loving father and husband. This is the man I grew up with and this is how I choose to remember him. I forgive Dad for not telling me the truth—in some way I understand how hard it must have been for him to live this double life.

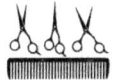

Salon Story

Lonely Gift Giver

One of my fussiest customers, yet one of my favorites, is a lady who was a customer for over fifteen years. She was always giving me jewelry, not costume either, but real diamonds and real pearls, some amazing pieces. She was so grateful that I was so kind to her all those years. You see, she was extremely hard to please and I would often stay late for her or come in early, and I never complained. I understood why she was the way she was and it was okay. She was so unhappy in her marriage, yet she stayed. Her husband was always traveling and often work would be more important than family. He was always buying her jewelry and she wasn't impressed. Some of the jewelry she gave to me, she said he would never notice it missing since she had so much. As strange as it sounds, I accepted the jewelry because it made her happy to give it to me. I had it appraised, four necklaces, one ring; over two thousand dollars. I guess it was strange to accept jewelry that a husband gave his wife, but I did.

Who is Gertrud Matejovic? (PT 2)?

About six months after Gertrud started her job at the pub in Salzburg, she met a handsome American Army officer. He was much older, but he was very kind to her and did not seem interested in the things that some of the other lower ranked soldiers were doing, such as getting drunk, being loud, and acting inappropriately toward the girls. As an officer, he turned a blind eye from holding them accountable or having them arrested.

Lloyd in Vienna circa 1947

Gertrud spoke very little English and he spoke little German; even so, they did form a close friendship over time. He came into the pub every day looking for her and gave her plentiful tips. She was quite taken by his good looks, his kindness and generosity, and his high rank as an officer. She knew he could be married, but his wife was thousands of miles away. Gertrud began to think of him as her ticket out of Austria. After about six months, they took their friendship to the next level and she invited him to her room with her for the night. Her first sexual experience was at barely sixteen years of age; he was gentle and sweet, helping her through every step, and that night she fell in love. She was young and naive and, after all, he was wonderful to her. Initially he thought of himself as simply having an affair, a wartime fling like most of his men, but after several months, he too was falling in love with her, an attractive young girl who would do anything he asked of her. Yes, he was smitten with Gertrud.

After that first year, Gertrud at sixteen and he thirty-seven, he wanted more time with Gertrud and he thought of ways to bring her to the shores of America as an aid worker so he could still be with her. He knew with his rank he could pull a few strings. Their love was growing, but soon this handsome officer had news, his wife was coming to Austria and they would live together till his tour of duty had ended.

Unwilling to give up Gertrud's love, he rented an apartment for them to continue being together. Gertrud felt her soldier would soon have to make a choice, and he would surely choose his wife over her. And Gertrud really had no one looking out for her except him. He knew if the affair was found out by his wife or the US Army, all hell would break loose, and he would not only lose his marriage, but he'd be court-martialed. Gertrud was a minor in the eyes of the law, but to him she was a woman in every way, the woman he loved, it was a passionate love for both of them. He had to make a plan; he had to keep Gertrud a secret, but how?

Gertrud was full of fear; she didn't want to go back to her life as a server at the inn, or turn tricks like Linda was doing, or live in that room above the inn in which she could hear other desperate, young Austrian women and young girls like herself giving their bodies to men in hopes of fulfilling a longing for a better life and support. She was in love, and she had never felt such love before. Her mother turned her out at fifteen, her sister was married, and her father had committed suicide. None of her relatives who were left could afford to help her or take her in, she was alone. The entire country was desperately hanging on as reconstruction took its time and inevitable toll on its innocent souls there. So many were depressed and suicide became commonplace as families were torn apart and businesses were wiped out. With no jobs or economy, their once thriving little town of Salzburg had again been destroyed by a war.

Soon to be seventeen, Gertrud tried to hold on to her handsome soldier, but knew it was only a matter of time before his work was done and he would be reassigned and return to America, with his wife, and without her. Linda told her to get out of the relationship because it was not going to end well and she would help her get a job and a place to stay as she had done before. The American soldier told her he still wanted to be with her, but she would have to understand the bind he was in. As long as his wife was in Austria, they would share housing and he emphasized firmly that the army could never find out about the affair. So, he started to take assignments to Vienna, where he had military housing provided there with his wife, and traveled back and forth from Salzburg to Vienna frequently.

His wife understood her husband's duties as an officer and never asked any questions. She was used to her husband having different assignments, being gone for extended periods, and she never questioned his absence. After all, they spoke daily on the phone.

This worked well until Gertrud found out she was carrying his child. This would change everything. Gertrud—terrified of being alone, poor, pregnant, and unmarried—didn't know how to tell him. He had already explained to her that the doctors told him that he and his wife couldn't bear children, but Gertrud knew she had to tell him before he discovered it for himself as her tummy got larger. He told her many times that he always wanted to be a father, but couldn't and by his late thirties, he gave up any thoughts about having children.

Gertrud finally told him she was going to have his child; by this time she was three months along. He was in shock at this unintended turn of events and needed another plan. He was both thrilled and terrified. He had to make a plan and not get caught by his wife or the military. This weighed very heavily on him.

Meanwhile, the soldier's wife was making her own plans—plans to go back to the States when he got a new assignment. The wife loved the army life as an officer's wife, and she loved her husband and made his life as an officer very enjoyable and comfortable. He took very good care of her too. As an army wife she knew he would be away for days or weeks at a time, even a year during their marriage; that is just part of the army life she had embraced for nearly two decades. She always knew he would come back to her, and he always did. He was just that kind of man, one who was devoted to her and took care of those whom he loved, and there was no doubt that he loved his wife and she loved him.

Gertrud never thought her soldier would stand by her during the pregnancy, but he did. However, he could not put his name on the birth records because he would have a big price to pay if he was found out, both by the army and his wife. After all, Gertrud was a minor, only seventeen and by law, he was breaking military orders just by being with her, he could lose his career. But there was a mutual love between them that could not be denied. Can you really love two women? It seemed that he did.

After the baby was born, Gertrud tried to care for her child, but was told by the hospital workers that since she was not married, did not have a job, and no way to support a baby, it would be better off if she gave her up for adoption. But Gertrud wanted to be a mother and refused to give her up.

She named her Hermine. She grew quickly, and at one year of age, Gertrud was still very much in love with her child and did not want to give her up. Although her lover was providing for them both, the officer and his wife were planning to go back to America as his tour of duty was coming to an end. Gertrud could not support a baby by herself, so the officer hatched a plan. He convinced her to surrender Hermine to an orphanage temporarily and he would try to help her by bringing them both to America for humanitarian reasons.

This started his great plan to deceive Gertrud as he never intended to bring her to America. He had to choose between two women. At this time, he just needed to get himself out of the relationship and make sure the child was cared for in the orphanage, because he knew that once he left Austria, Gertrud would no longer have his financial support. This grieved him deeply. He did love her and his child, but if found out, he would be court-martialed.

Gertrud had to trust and believe her lover's plan. So he had her take Hermine to an orphanage, but told Gertrud it was only temporary. After Gertrud surrendered Hermine to the youth welfare authority, she visited her every day and waited for news about when both of them would go to America. She thought her officer was arranging this for her. But after six months, news never came from him about going to America and more time passed.

She continued to visit each week as Hermine grew older. Now at two years old, she had been in the orphanage one year. Unbeknownst to Gertrud, a couple from Venezuela applied to adopt little Hermine. Gertrud was told nothing about this impending adoption; she thought Hermine was on temporary hold waiting for her mother to come for her and take her home, and Gertrud never signed any papers permitting her daughter to be adopted to Venezuela. All she was told was that her daughter became a legal ward of the state because of the length of time Hermine was left there, until further arrangements could be made. Gertrud had no legal counsel or any real understanding of what was to happen to her daughter. She began to worry if she was ever going to get her baby back or go to America. She was still seeing her lover who continued to reassure her he was making good on his promises, and he was also visiting Hermine as often as he could without raising suspicions.

More months went by and the little girl was growing, becoming charming, talking, and more attached to her parents. Hermine remained at the orphanage six more months, thinking she had no hope of leaving with her parents. The orphanage had become her home now and her parents, only visitors.

One day when Gertrud came for her weekly visit, she was told Hermine was gone—adopted out. Gertrud was shocked, dismayed, and heartbroken. Knowing that she never signed for her daughter to be put up for adoption, she thought Hermine was put in foster care of the state, that she could have her back anytime she wanted when she could prove she could support her. That was the story she was always told. After Hermine was taken, Gertrud went to the Red Cross, the embassy, the military offices, anywhere she could to find out where Hermine was taken, but no one would give her answers about where she went.

And her lover was gone too. Did he leave without saying goodbye or coming for her as he had promised? It seems that is exactly what happened. She cried every day, pining for the daughter who was stolen from her. No one would disclose who adopted her. Did she go to Venezuela after all? Gertrud was full of grief and questions but not getting any answers, and she was falling into a deep depression.

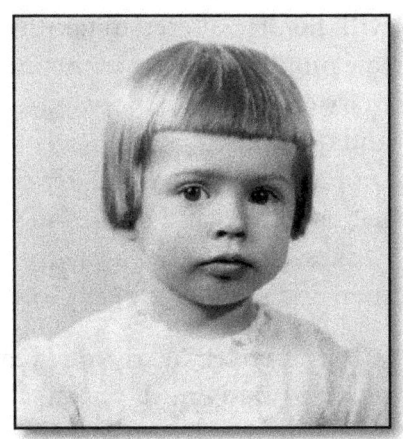

Hermine in Austrian orphanage, 2.5 yrs, 1951

All the adoption papers were sealed. How was this possible without a mother's permission? Gertrud became more and more depressed and felt very lost. Her dreams of a better life faded quickly. She was now nineteen, still very young and now very much alone. She would have to leave the apartment her lover paid for and look for work and a place to stay. This would not be easy, she felt betrayed by a man she trusted and loved.

Alone without Hermine or her lover, she returned to the inn and the only friend she had, Linda. Gertrud had to make money and her friend showed her how to get it. Gertrud became a prostitute herself, and fell deeper and deeper into despair. She continued her life as a prostitute and met a man several years later, one of her regulars who had fallen in love with her. He offered to take her out of prostitution after only a few months of being with her; she agreed and they were later married. Mr. Kainer owned a supply barge and traveled up and down the Danube River selling a wide range of shipping supplies for companies. For the first time in years, Gertrud felt happiness and reveled in it, letting her hardships and sadness drift farther away from her. Mr. Kainer was a good man and seemed to really love and care for her.

They enjoyed nearly four years of wedded bliss and partnership, until one day as the boat was coming in to port, Mr. Kainer jumped off to secure the barge to the dock like he had done for many years. Only this time he fell and hit his head on the barge. He called out to Gertrud immediately, and she held him in her arms as he bled to death. Soaked in his blood, she kissed him, in disbelief that another dream for security was suddenly shattered.

Once again, Gertrud was left devastated, broken, and alone. If you were not married or supported by a family or a husband, a young widow had a hard time making ends meet. She could not run the barge herself and had to sell the business to fend for herself. Soon she returned to prostitution, the only job she knew could support her. Sinking deeper into depression, having lost her family, her lover, two children and her husband, she saw no way out until a year later when another one of her johns paid to just sit and talk with her. Most of the Johns did not hold conversations, but this man was lonely.

He told her his wife was dying in a hospital and he was lonely, not for sex, but for companionship. He saw something good in Gertrud that she could not see for herself. So, for one long year, Johann came and paid to talk with Gertrud. He came every week, two to three times, for one to two hours at each visit. She told Johann that she hated what she had become, and she wanted out. She even talked about ending her own life. He wanted her to stop turning tricks for other men and be with him only. He told her he would not leave her, but he was still married and could not help her financially until his wife died; she had been ill for years.

Gertrud didn't believe Johann would wait for her—her heart had grown cold—but she continued to allow him to see her. Later that same year Johann's wife did die. Finally, Gertrud agreed to leave prostitution. Johann made good on his promise and Gertrud never turned another trick again. At twenty-eight, Gertrud finally left prostitution and never looked back. Could she finally find the strength to love herself and the person she was, and be happy with Johann?

Today

Today, Gertrud lives with Johann in a small village in a remote area of Austria, thirty miles outside of Salzburg in a quiet town called Ostermiething where they have a dog, grow vegetables, drink coffee, drive around in an old Jeep, and enjoy a very lovely, quiet, and private life. I visited them and saw for myself how their love has lasted and how they take good care of each other and live a modest life. Gertrud told me that Johann is a good man, but her heart was not repaired from her past completely. I could see the forty-plus years of grief etched on her face and the sorrow of never being my mother. The face of a broken woman who tried so hard to survive a life she never wanted to lose. She relives that lifetime of shame and guilt daily and she told me she wasn't even worthy of stepping into a church because of her sins. Shame overcomes her daily life. I asked her if she would please go to church with me; she resisted at first, but after a few hours she did walk with me to a Sunday Mass down the street.

The church was breathtakingly beautiful and very ornate as Catholic churches are in Austria, full of history and traditions. As we got closer, she started to shake with fear and her body trembled as I held her up as we entered. I told her that I love to sit near the front when I normally attend church, but she pulled me to the back and told me she was not worthy to sit any closer; that the good people sat in the front and the poor and those who had led sinful lives sat in the back, so everyone knew them. They were seen as shameful lost souls looking for forgiveness.

After about fifteen minutes, she started to cry silent tears and shake with more intensity. It hurt me that she felt such deep shame and sorrow.

Without warning, she ran out of the church. I followed her and we walked home quietly together holding hands. She had suffered more than I could have imagined. It made me so sad. I told her that her sins were forgiven and she doesn't have to carry that shame or guilt anymore, but she simply said she had to; it had become a way of life for her. My heart wept as I held her as we both cried silent tears. I told her I forgave her and I had turned out okay, that my life was good in America.

I knew I had to withhold much of the truth of my abusive childhood; it might have depressed her more. She had suffered long enough. She carried deep shame and such a sense of loss. She didn't seem to have any joy; it was only Johann who made her laugh now.

I was with her for my birthday and she made me a birthday cake and told me it was the first one she had ever made. She baked it from scratch. We ate it and laughed and held hands. She gave me a few gifts such as assorted cowbells and a beautiful beer stein. I treasure those gifts today.

Her lifetime of grief also affected her health. I found out a year after my visit that she had Parkinson's disease and could no longer write to me. Her hands shook and her balance was off. She moved from their home in Ostermiething to receive better care.

She requested that I not look for her again but to keep good memories in my heart from our visit together. I did try to find her, but all my letters were returned, and sadly we have not corresponded since the end of 1997.

The news was very sad for me as I could no longer write, call, or visit her in Austria again. He is an honorable man and he loves her very much. It has been twenty-one years since my visit to Austria and more than nineteen since I received my first letter from Gertrud, my dear mother, as she called herself my "real mother." It was so cute. I pray for her and I ask for my healing also from the years of separation from the woman who always wanted me and the broken heart she carries with her to this day from losing me.

I know God has forgiven all her sins, I just wish she could forgive herself as I so easily have forgiven her. She asked me when I left her if I could find the son she gave up when she was a prostitute. I said I would. While still in Austria, we went to the house of records at a huge municipal building near Mirabell Plaza, a beautiful place where all the recorded documents of the people of Austria were kept in what they call the "big books."

Every child who was ever born in Austria was recorded there. You cannot take photos, or any documents with you, only make notes, everything stays there. I saw my name and where I was born and I did find my birth record, but, as I saw it in my documents at home from Mom's lock box, it read, "father unknown." That spoke volumes to me.

One year after my visit to see Gertrud, I did find my half-brother in a state prison in Arizona. I spoke with his lawyer and he told me that his birth name became his middle name, that his adoptive mother was very controlling and his adopted father had died. He was adopted into an American military family as a baby from Austria.

I contacted his adoptive mother, and found out that my half-brother was very intelligent but didn't take care of himself very well; a little strange and self-centered. I knew I could never have a relationship with him, though I corresponded with him during his last year in prison.

My first contact with Robert, or Wolfgang as was his birth name, was very formal and the letters that followed got more and more strange, to the point that I feared him and felt threatened. I was told by his lawyer that he was not violent, but mentally unstable. He was in prison for fraud and had a genius-level IQ. He was very manipulative and thought of himself too highly.

I told Robert (Wolfgang) that I had found and visited our mother, and he got very angry and told me he wanted nothing to do with her and he cursed her in his heart every day. It was awful to hear and very sad too. Apparently he never felt his adoption was a good thing, he focused more on the rejection of his birth mother and never allowed me to explain her reasons for giving him up.

I called Gertrud with the sad news that Robert wanted nothing to do with her, and she barely could speak. In her broken English, she thanked me and asked me to be careful of him. I told her it was okay, that we could not change his hard heart and not to blame herself. The next year was the year she moved and I never spoke or heard from her again.

As for my half-brother, he continued to write me many strange letters till he got out of prison. I got a call from the warden at the prison the month before his release warning me that he might come to California to see me. So threatening was he at the time that I was advised to relocate and change my name. I was concerned for myself and my kids, but not really afraid of him. I appreciated the warning and took the advice. I lived a more careful life after he was released. I did move and remarry, which effectively changed my name. My sons are grown and no longer with me, so I am not concerned anymore for them. I am thankful that I never allowed fear to control my life. I never searched for Wolfgang again, nor has he searched for me or written to me again. I am okay with that. I fulfilled the promise I made to Gertrud.

I was told Robert's adopted mother died while he was locked up in his last year of prison and that he always knew about me; I don't know how, he never explained, but his mother, Genevieve, did tell me in a phone conversation that they did know Robert had a half-sister who was adopted out before he was born. I got a postcard from his mother asking for confirmation about me. As strange as that was, it was never fully explained to me. Both of our adoptive fathers were in the military.

That chapter was closed, sealed, never to be relived again. I still have some of his very strange letters; I guess I will get rid of them one day. I am not sure why I kept all of them, but I have. I never revisit any of the letters and I really have no desire to. Some things are just better left alone. Yet for some reason, I just still cannot let go of the letters. Maybe it is still that one birth connection.

I saw clearly how Gertrud had been duped, lied to, and treated badly all her life and my heart breaks for her, but nothing can be done now but to pray for her and my half-brother. I am glad she never knew how badly I was treated as a child and I am glad I came through life okay too. Forgiveness is powerful and healing for our souls.

I have been asked often if finding the truth set me free, and really it has in many ways. But often, the truth can devastate you, confuse you, sadden you, turn your world upside down, and cause great pain. I believe that how you handle that truth is what really sets you free. For me, I have great faith and I was determined, no matter what I found out, that I was not going to allow my emotions to rule my life. I learned forgiveness, compassion and what real love looks like along my journey of discovery. These are the things that set me free. Absolute truth is a good thing; no matter what the truth is, we still choose how we will deal with it. I choose to love and forgive at all times and with all the people who have come in and out of my life.

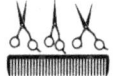

Salon Story

Hairdresser on Wheels

I created a mobile hair business in Tulsa, Oklahoma and went to nursing homes and rehabilitation centers to fix and wash hair for those who couldn't go to a salon. I started building a good client base and the families were all very grateful for my services. One client that was most memorable was an older lady in a hospital. As I approached the hospital, I was told I had to park in the visitor's parking, about a quarter of a mile from the door I needed to use. So I parked far away and unloaded a stand-up dryer, a huge case with my supplies, and my purse which seemed like extra luggage to me. So on I went through the parking lot with my arms loaded. I got to the door and a nice man coming out said, "Oh, you have your hands full, do you need help?" I replied that I did, but that I was going to the third floor. He said he was happy to help and he didn't mind escorting me because he was going that way too.

As we walked, he told me he was there to visit his mom who was in bad shape and asked if I would pray for her. "Of course," I said. He seemed very sad at the thought of losing his mom so I tried to encourage him. I told him I was a mobile hairdresser and asked if his mother needed my services. He said thanks, but she sleeps all the time till the aides get her up. I could tell how loving he felt toward his mom. It made me feel good to see a son so close to his mother. It reminded me of my caring sons who are always checking on me and making sure I'm okay.

I finally got to my client's room on the third floor. She was very heavy and could only sit up in a wheelchair. With help, we got her from the bed to the chair but getting her into the bathroom was another story. The room was handicapped accessible, but to get her near enough to the tiny sink and sitting her backwards was nearly impossible. She couldn't bend her neck very far back on my shampoo board, so I had to use a cup to bring the water to her head as she basically had to sit straight up. Pretty soon I was wet, she was wet, and the floor was flooded. It was a real mess. An aide had to come in to mop up the floor and change her. When she was assisted back into the wheelchair, I cut and styled her hair. What was normally a thirty-minute procedure took ninety minutes and I was still wet when I left, but felt I made a lovely contribution to how she felt about herself.

TRECHO

Trecho: This is a Greek word meaning to make a journey; speed ahead.

This story has been a journey and at times it seems to speed up! People say that time flies. If this is true, the journey in our lives should never end. I guess it depends on how you travel; fast, slow, or on pause. We experience fear, love, joy, and tragedy. All these things have a way of making our journeys unique. The people that come and go, the situations that are before us, and how we handle all life's challenges will determine how we travel on this journey. For me, many of life's moments have taken curves and hit speed bumps.

Emotionally, I have moved faster than I wanted; physically, I think I still have scars. I was told in massage school that every cell in our body holds an emotion, good or bad. Tiny cells hold onto things we aren't even aware of. So I guess this proves that physically we have a journey and emotionally we also have a journey. Each journey in life brings us new things to explore. Whether we speed up or take things slower, we will all learn things about ourselves.

I have also been told that our problems amount to only 10 percent of the real issues, but how we react to them covers the other 90 percent of our perceived problems. It is in this that we can change our journey. Our life needs balance; the one thing I didn't have. My journey led me to meet many people, see many places, and discover many things along the way. Some things I blocked out for a long time. They were too painful for my mind to recall them. Some things I remember very clearly and need more understanding, and still search how to cope with them. My childhood memories were not all joyful, but my search to turn things around has been my driving force on this journey. The joyful memories seemed to be on full throttle, fast and few, and I embraced them and let go of the other stuff that kept me in standstill mode. Family vacations were fun as were school field trips. Visiting my aunt in Florida was something I always looked forward to and remember as joyful.

Time also sped by when I became a hairdresser, a career that I have found much joy in. Being a mother, I have had both joy and sadness, and that time sped by quickly also. Being married nineteen years moved fast, although the last five years of it seemed to crawl as the marriage broke apart.

My hunt for who I became was another journey in itself. I have a professional career, I'd been a wife, a business owner, a friend, a mother, and wore many hats. I guess my journey was mostly curvy during those times. And although I would not change a thing, I would like to slow down a bit.

The journey I chose was finding out who I really was created to be. For that, I looked for biblical solutions. Who is this great big God and why did I have the journey that I had and where do I go from here? In 1993, I started going with a friend to her church, I was seeking to know myself better. I guess you could say I wanted to know how God sees me and my life. I never wanted to join a cult or a religion or get wacky in my search, but later I looked for a Bible school that simply taught the Bible. The King James version was the only Bible I had, but it was hard to understand on my own. I met some people in that church that had a Bible study in a home and I was asked to join in. I was hesitant but I knew these people rather well so I went. The leader was well-versed in his teachings and we used the King James and a concordance, which made it easier to understand the meanings of some Greek and Hebrew wordings.

It was then that my spiritual journey started. In that one year alone, I got very excited at what I discovered, and I wanted to go to Bible school just as our teacher had, so I enrolled and started a plan. For the first time in my life I felt connected to my emotional and physical self. The journey was still a bit curvy but less fearful. People would tell me often, "Let go and trust God," but I did not understand how to let go and trust a God I did not know. This journey was certainly a process. It was my choice to sell my business; and leave my life in California, John, my friends, church, and everything I had known for twenty-three years.

After my house was taken from me through bad business decisions my ex-husband made, I divorced. Simultaneously, my son's bipolar disease was really getting him in trouble. I was looking for a way out; I was ready for a new journey. I had already found my birth mother, and gone to Austria to discover why my childhood was full of lies and painful memories, so it was time for a complete change, a new journey of self-discovery, just for me and not anyone else.

Have you ever thought of doing that? Just bailing out of your life as it is? I have many times, and this time at fifty-two years of age I was ready. Everything I had worked hard for and the years of building a life was over; it was time for the next chapter. My house was gone, I got nothing for it; my business was strong but I turned it over to someone else to run, and my church that started me on my journey was supportive. As for my resale shop, I donated everything to a women's shelter, it was all so freeing, but it left me broke and trusting God.

I felt free, yet a bit nervous. I was always a keep your feet on solid ground type of person and to just pick up and move to a place that I knew no one and had no job or support was a bit strange and out of character for me, but somehow I was at peace. Is that how you feel when you are trusting God? I hope so. My younger son Daniel who was nineteen at that time wanted to go with me to Tulsa, Oklahoma; he was ready for a journey too, but was afraid for me to go off somewhere unknown and felt protective of me. I found his heart tender and caring to want to come with me on this journey, it was endearing and he did help me. I got an apartment sight unseen near the school. I prepaid rent and school fees for three months, thinking I would find a job and income by then.

I saved money for six months prior to my giving up my salon and leaving. I rented a truck, stuffed it full, and my son and his friend drove the truck while I followed in my car. I thought I would follow the truck and keep an eye on my stuff and my son, but a two-day drive got us separated in the small towns and stopping to eat and gas up. I don't even like to drive really and to be alone on my second day driving was a bit scary, but again, I had a peace I couldn't fully explain to myself. I was in touch by cell phone with Daniel and his friend, but there was nowhere that I could see them or give them money, they had to figure out how to get to Oklahoma on their own with the money we started with. This was his journey and he wasn't even scared. He had never traveled across country alone, but he seemed okay with all of it. Was he trusting God too? I am not sure; you would have to ask him.

I arrived at my destination on the third day, tired and concerned about my son and in a place that I knew no one. I met my new landlord and got the key to my apartment. It was in a historic home that was divided into three units and I had the largest space on the ground floor. It was old, just one furnace in the floor to heat the entire apartment. The washer and dryer would have to be set up separately, the washer outside in a storage space and the dryer inside in a hallway.

It was getting late and still the truck full of furniture and my son had not arrived and I was worried they might be lost. I didn't have good cell service and my calls often got dropped when I called Daniel. I went to the Bible school to check in and to meet some people. At this time I was concerned if I had done the right thing by picking up and leaving my stable environment for the unknown. The first person I met was an older man, Dale, who was also checking in. He introduced himself and I told him I needed prayer because my son was driving a truck and we had gotten separated and he was out of money. I thought since I was at a Bible school that maybe other people had more faith than I did. Maybe God would listen to them better than me! Haha.

He said sure, let's gather up a few more people and form a circle and pray. They bowed their heads and beautiful words were flowing. I looked around and they were really praying and concerned about my son; they were complete strangers. I was amazed, and peace passed over me.

My cell phone rang the minute we stopped praying. It was Daniel; he was about two hours away at a gas station out of gas and money. He asked if I could come to him. I told the prayer group my son was stranded at a gas station and Dale said, "I will take you, I can help."

Wow! Really, I couldn't believe this kind gesture. He then said, let's pray for this one more time, and they prayed that angels would look after Daniel and the truck and bring him help. That sounded good to me. As we started to get into Dale's truck, the phone rang, it was Daniel again, a complete stranger had offered to fill the truck with gas, about sixty dollars worth. So I didn't need to go and he was only two hours away and all was well. Wow, that prayer thing really worked. I was more excited about God than ever before.

When Daniel arrived a few hours later, even he was amazed at a total stranger being genuinely concerned, filling up the truck, and making sure he was headed the right way. I guess we both felt blessed that day. Dale helped us unload the truck and set up the utilities. We were finally at our new destination but the journey was far from over.

Dale became a good friend and helped us move in and get settled at the school. He was looking out for me and I liked it! A total stranger reaching out to help was wonderful. It was strictly a friendship; he was a gentleman in every way. A great way to start a new life!

Daniel got a job right away and I started school and looked for a job. I could only work around school hours, so my chance for salon work was limited. It is the only career I ever had and really, I didn't have many other skills. I took a giant leap of faith after what I had witnessed when I first got there and posted a job request on the school community board.

Daniel brought in our only income, and at $7.50 an hour, we got just enough with his overtime to pay for rent and food. This was the first time in my life that I wasn't the support of my family; I was never without a job or money until now. I was getting nervous, but tried to stay calm believing something good was going to come. I guess that was called having faith. I was still new at this trusting God thing.

After the first month, we were scraping bottom, most of what I saved was gone and there was really no job in sight yet for me. My career is mostly commission-based or booth rental, but I was looking for salary. In the second month, I got a call saying someone saw my ad on the school board and wanted to interview me. We only had one car, so I had to make sure I could go when Daniel was working, so that I could drop him off, go to school, and then meet with this woman.

She gave me the address of her salon and I couldn't believe it. It was one block from my apartment and I could walk. And the school was only three blocks. Suddenly I had no car issues. I was excited to go to the salon and find out if she would hire me. Her name was Pam and she had graduated from the Bible school I was attending, and often looked for students to help out. We hit it off and I was hired and given a booth. I was starting with commission and she would help me get clients. She had a busy salon, very small, only three of us and a nail tech, and everyone had attended the school I was attending.

It took several months until I was actually making money and I had to have faith and trust God that things would get better, and things did get better. I started meeting people and making friends and I got involved with programs at the church prison ministry, the Sunday school, and became a teacher assistant with fifth graders. Things were going well.

And then I met my current husband who had moved there from Houston, Texas. He was on the same kind of journey I was.

We became friends, then things got more serious and I knew he would be with me for a long time.

Daniel stood up with me at our wedding in 2003. They got along great and still do. We served in the prison ministry and in the Sunday children's school, as well as Bible studies, and two years of the school program. I learned who God really is and how He sees me. It was revolutionary and a pivotal change in my life and journey. I learned about love, the very thing I had searched for all my life, real love, in your heart, a love that remains.

This is the peace that has stayed with me for twelve years since attending Bible school. I still had difficult days ahead, but now I saw a different way to deal with them. My journey is not over and I am more excited than ever. I have moved away from Oklahoma and the school, but I took something with me I never had before, a greater understanding of my purpose and who I really am. And yes, I learned how to "let go and trust God." The friends I met along the way are still a part of my life. Even though I don't stay in touch anymore and have moved away, they are forever in my heart and prayers, and I am thankful for each one.

The journey is not over, and the next chapter in life has more for me to learn and do, and I welcome it. It has sped up but I do have fewer curves and speed bumps. I have focus, love, and joy, all things I never had as a child. I still do not have all the answers but I do know how to get them!

Reflections

I believe Vera loved my dad and was completely happy not having children for eighteen years of their marriage. Vera was the wife, best friend, supporter, cheerleader, and lover to my dad. Once she found out about Dad's infidelity, it shattered her heart to the core. Hate crept in, not for Dad, but for his betrayal and toward anyone who was a part of that betrayal. Love didn't die immediately when Vera found out, but over the years to come, it did, and hate, anger, and distrust took over. She just couldn't get past the betrayal and see a child who needed two parents to love her. That is sad, but it's a fact.

I have heard people say, "I would have rather not known" but really, truth always brings an action. Living a lie, to me, is worse. I think Vera just wanted to look away and build her life around Dad and not have to deal with her real emotions. When truth comes, you better be ready for it, good or bad. Truth is always better because your emotions can lead you to a very unhappy life.

For me as a young child, my truth was, Vera didn't like me, or love me, but I never knew why. It was that question I asked myself all my life, till I found truth, and then I understood Vera. I was mad at Dad for the lies we all had to live with and I was sad that Vera had to harden her heart toward me, but truth helped me see love in its raw form. Vera was so devastated from Dad's betrayal that she lost all sight of love. Her love was built over eighteen years of devotion to her husband and the military as an army wife, her love was for one man and one way of life.

I think she accepted long ago that she was never going to have children and poured all her love into her husband. She trusted her marriage, her husband, and for eighteen years, her life was everything she wanted it to be. She loved her adopted son, but because of her dislike for her daughter and what she reminded her of, she lived in a battle with love and hate.

Hate took over and it nearly destroyed her. Vera could still display some love to her husband and her son but the hate kept her from peace in her heart and really loving any of them deeply. Love has to be in you, deep inside you, it is not superficial or transparent, it is seen in your actions and daily living. Human knowledge is fragmentary, incomplete and imperfect, but when the complete, real love comes, the incomplete will vanish away. In the eyes of Vera, her love vanished when she had to deal with her disappointment and betrayal of the one person she truly loved, Dad. She tried to hold onto that love, but as time went by even that faded away. Her heart became hardened, bitter, and it replaced that love she once had.

Through the eyes of a child, I saw this love die and no joy remained. Vera put up a good front because she never wanted anyone to know her truth or her failures. But acting is not always a way back to love. An actress is only putting on a show for others, and usually people could see truth better than the actress. I grew up acting normal, but feeling the truth of Vera's hate and resentment, yet never knowing the truth till after her death. Now forgiveness replaces hurt in my heart and peace is able to rule over me. I am able to love my children and my husband, as well as close friends, deeply. I often stay away from angry, hurting people because I do not wish to be drawn in by the negative energy that hurt me growing up. I choose to love and look for the good in all people. I see truth and I choose to love my way through everything that comes. I longed to feel love and be loved my whole life, but now I am at total peace with love and fully understand what it is and what it isn't. Once you see how much love can move you to great things and be in you, the more peace it brings you.

I am married again; completed Bible school with straight As and still thrive as a hairdresser here in North Carolina while helping care for my mother-in-law who is ninety-four years young. My life forever changed when I learned how much I could be loved and how great my God is. My past is my past, but it did not break me. I thank my father for his leadership and raising me to always take the good with the bad. He never spoke unkindly about me, and unfortunately, he missed out on my life as a wife, mother and businesswoman. He would have liked the woman I have become and I pray one day I will see him in heaven.

Loss & Learning

Through the years, most of my family has died, and these losses taught me a great deal about spending time loving the family I have with me in this moment.

Robbie died in 1992 from a heroin overdose. He left a wife and two teenage children who tried to love him and help him, but Robbie was stuck in a world only he knew. I got a call at 4:30 in the morning from a coroner in San Diego, California. He had my brother's body there and wanted me to verify that it was him. I described his snake tattoo that went all the way up and around his arm with the snake's head on Robbie's shoulder. It was very distinct and unmistakable. The man said, "Yes, this is Robert."

I had another funeral to plan. Now they are all gone, and oddly enough I never got to speak to any of them before their deaths. Maybe it was better that way, though I still live with unanswered questions.

The next year, my brother-in-law Jack died; he was forty-two years of age. I didn't have the capacity to cry anymore; I just went through the motions, numbly doing whatever had to be done for another proper burial ceremony. I buried all four grandparents, both parents, cousins, and now my brother and brother-in-law before I turned forty-five. I was numb with grief. I often wondered how I could go on without breaking down. I had to focus on the future with my children. The kids were a wonderful distraction from the deep grief I experienced for so long.

Remember my Auntie Lyn? Well, I did visit with her three weeks before she died, and it was wonderful. We laughed and we wept, she was always on my side and I know she loved me—I was at peace knowing her and seeing her before she passed away. Auntie Lyn was the first to plant the seed in my heart and show me that love was possible.

I have one cousin, Lyn's son, who lives in Florida. We do chat from time to time. Interestingly enough, he was adopted too!

Remember that giving your home to a child in need is an awesome thing, no matter how you choose to adopt a child, but be ready emotionally and financially, and in your heart and marriage. This couple is in a solid, loving marriage. If you already have children, make your adopted child feel like he or she was always supposed to be yours, not a rescue project, but a gift to your family. Expect the same love and respect from an adopted child as you do your birth children. Above all, love and accept them knowing there will be differences. If you do decide to adopt internationally, know the ways of that country, get information on medical and family history if possible, visit and spend time with that child, make sure you can take on any problems and that you will be able to love and care for them always.

Unusual Gifts

For some reason, clients and other people seemed to always be giving me gifts. My birthday was always remembered by my regular clients, as well as Christmas and other occasions.

In the building where I had my salon in North Monterrey, California, I leased space to run a resale and gift store. Lots of wonderful things passed in and out of my doors. I had customers who gave me some of their personal jewelry, beautiful coats, mink jackets, and also my wedding dress. It is my wedding dress that I want to tell you about.

I had been given several wedding dresses to sell, but on this occasion one of my regular customers came in and pulled me aside. She asked if I would accept her wedding dress, not to sell, but to keep. Well, I was divorced and not really serious with anyone and I thought it odd that she would make such an offer, but I accepted it with much gratitude. I knew she had married the love of her life in it and I felt honored. She told me I would meet the right man someday and this dress would be perfect. It is an old fashioned A-line dress, satin and antique lace with a huge bustling bow in the back. It is ivory, and had a pillbox lace hat and long laced gloves. It was really beautiful, oh and it was my size, a size six. Okay, I was barely able to fit into a six.

It was about two years later that I felt a tug on my heart to move and go to Bible school in Oklahoma. I had put the dress in a small gym bag and forgot all about it; after all, I had no need for a wedding dress at that time. I registered for Bible school, found an apartment close by and saved money to move to Oklahoma with my son Daniel. My friends and customers whom I adored were shocked.

I sold my shop, packed a rental truck, and we left. We knew no one in Oklahoma but I was determined to go. The gym bag went with me, but not on purpose, my son had thrown it on the truck. I gave away all my resale clothing to a woman's shelter and off we went.

The first year at school I met a dashing, tall man who was in his second year at the school. It was not love at first sight, more like a friendly attraction. Kevin was very kind and helpful, showing me around. He offered to take me to get a blood test, which he also needed to work in the prison ministry during Bible school. We went to lunch afterward. You could say that soon we ended up in prison together—doing good, of course, and getting to know each other better.

Toward the end of my first year, I could clearly see Kevin was going to be my husband. So when he asked me to marry him on Valentine's Day in 2003, I accepted and said, "Great, I already have a dress!" He looked stunned, but we both had a good laugh. Not having money for a ring, Kevin bought two praying hands pins and we pinned each other and considered ourselves engaged until we married in June of 2003. We did want rings but could not afford them yet.

In the paper a few days later, I saw an ad that said, "Will pay four hundred dollars for one overnight stay on a test plane. Call this number." Okay, I thought, this is a great way to get a fast eight hundred dollars for the rings, so I called the number and Kevin and I went for one whole night on a flight simulator that was testing cabin pressure. Needless to say, we were not prepared to nearly lose consciousness as they depleted the air in the cabin to see how potential passengers would respond. Every ten minutes throughout the evening and overnight, the organizers asked us questions to gauge our states of alertness. As time went on, we became too lethargic to answer clearly and just wanted to sleep. To make matters worse, there was not a bathroom to speak of. There was a camping commode with a curtain in front of it. So we were partially exposed while we relieved ourselves. It was quite an adventure. At least they fed us and we got the $800 for one night's work.

And we were able to get our rings. Kevin took care of all the wedding plans and I took care of the flowers and myself. We were married in Texas where Kevin was living before Bible school and where he was part of a very large church and ministry. I had that beautiful dress and somehow my customer knew I would use it! Thanks, Debbie.

Adoption: Provision versus Love

[Paraphrased from The Amplified Bible] 1 Cor 13:4-11

- Love endures long
- Love is patient and kind
- Love never is envious or boils over with jealousy
- Love is not boastful or vainglorious and does not display itself haughtily
- Love is not conceited or arrogant, or inflated with pride
- Love is not rude
- Love (God's love in us) does not insist on his own way or his own rights
- Love is not self-seeking, fretful, or resentful
- Love takes no account of evil done to us, and pays no attention to a suffered wrong
- Love does not rejoice in injustice and unrighteousness
- Love rejoices in right and truth

- Love bears up under anything and everything that comes

- Love is ever ready to believe the best of every person, its hopes are fadeless under all circumstances, and endures everything without weakening

- Love never fails or fades out, or becomes obsolete, or comes to an end.

- Knowledge will pass away; it will lose its value and be superseded by truth. Our knowledge is fragmentary, incomplete, imperfect; the complete and incomplete and imperfect will vanish away.

Definition of Provision according to Webster's Collegiate Dictionary: Being provided for; making some condition; provisional; conditional or temporary; preparing or providing, something provided for the future; preparatory measures taken in advance; i.e. legal document stipulating some specific thing; supply with provision, i.e. food, pending permanent arrangement, as a provisional government.

Adoption and Provision

To provide means simply to make preparations to take care of something or someone. Provision by itself is in no way the full expression of love. You can provide a good home but without love, it means nothing.

An animal at the SPCA is cared for, fed, walked, receives medical care, and their needs to sustain life are provided, but with so many animals, can each one be loved? The same can be said about overcrowded orphanages. These children need care, but they also need love.

To simply provide what is necessary is not enough. They need nurturing, to be held, given kindness, compassion, and told they are loved. Just like animals, children were also given up for adoption. Each child and animal is looking to be loved, accepted, and cared for.

The SPCA has requirements before you can adopt, and fees to pay. Human adoption also has requirements and fees to pay. In both of these adoptions, preparations are needed.

In human adoption, there are many ways to adopt and benefits to adopting. Are you really prepared? What documents will the IRS Adoption Tax Credit require? Are you looking at adoption for a tax break?

The documentation required will depend on the type of adoption that is right for you and whether the adoption can be finalized or not. Whether or not your child is considered special needs will also be a factor. This documentation is very important, so be sure that you have kept an adoption file folder and maintained various documents and receipts along your adoption journey.

In order to claim the IRS Adoption Tax Credit, you will need to show proof. Keep in mind that the documents you need will vary based on the type of adoption, and if the adoption is final. Check with a professional tax preparer before filing.

For example, you may need:

- receipts for adoption expenses
- final decree, or order of adoption
- entry visas for international adoptions
- home study by placement agency
- determination of special-needs status of the child

Note: These documents will need to be attached to your federal tax return.

An adoption specialist will work closely with adoptive parents to understand exactly the type of family you are looking for, based on race, age, religion, location, family size and much more.

Work with professional and certified agencies when considering adoption. They will help you navigate the system and adopt a child that is a good fit for your family.

Adoption specialists understand the type of family you are interested in, and you will be sent a selection of print profiles (either online or in the mail) with families that best match your adoption plan. The family profile provides a great deal of information about the adoptive family, such as their desire to become parents, their interests and hobbies, their house and neighborhood, and much more.

Video profiles allow the birth mother, who is giving her child up, to see an adoptive family in their home environment doing things they enjoy with friends and family. She can gain insight into how her child may become part of their family. She also gets an inside view of personalities and family characteristics.

Final note on provision

Provision became unimportant to me as I grew up. Let me explain. I was always able to work and provide for myself but without love, I was empty. The lesson learned was that you can have everything provided but without love, it is of no real value. Every child needs to have both, provision and love. It is my opinion that if you want to adopt, be sure you desire to give a child both love and provision. Make provision and be motivated by love to adopt, no matter which method you choose in finding a child. I also know parents who have adopted older children, never be afraid to adopt an older child and love them too! People have asked me if a child needs two parents, could a single person raise a happy well-cared-for child? Yes, but make sure you're prepared to answer all their questions as they get older and always make sure your child has provision and also love. A loved child will become a loving adult and later, a loving parent. I always knew things weren't right or fair, but I always hoped things would get better and they have!

Adoption Testimonials

Whether you are or are not considering adoption, this section will give you some insight through families who have agreed to share their adoption experiences.

All the stories are true, but the names of those who so generously shared their stories with me to share with you have been changed to protect their identity, and in some cases, their safety as well. Somewhere in these testimonials you might find yourself identifying with them—you are not alone.

Sandra's Story

Sandra and her husband could not bear children of their own, and after ten years of trying, they decided to adopt instead. They checked into adoption both in the US and in other countries. They were in their late thirties and did not want an infant, but rather an older child of two or three years. Older children are harder to place; most couples want a newborn or a very young baby. Sandra and her husband started the adoption process in the US and it took many months and much invasion of their privacy—such as home checks and interviews—but after two years, a young girl became available.

Her name was Jennifer; they liked her name, so they kept it and called her Jenny. She was shy, a little over four years old and had been in foster care since her birth. They knew very little about Jenny, only that her birth mother was very young and could not raise her. No medical records or family history was made available, just a name of the birth mother.

Sandra and Rick thought it would be better not to know too much, that way they could make their own family history with Jenny and not get clouded with secrets or sadness that they might have to reveal later in her life. Jenny was a bright, creative, and lively child, but it took a few years for her to settle in with her new parents. Jenny came from foster care in another state and little information was collected and passed along about this beautiful little girl they had adopted.

Four years after Jenny joined their family, Sandra became ill. She was thirty-eight and concerned enough to see a doctor. The shock of her life came when she tested positive for pregnancy. Sandra, who was told in her twenties that she could not have children, was pregnant. Feeling both shock and wonder at the miracle of it, Sandra and Rick prepared for a child of their own.

Michael was born when Jenny was eight years old. She knew she would soon have a brother, but didn't expect things to change as much as they did. As an infant, Michael required a lot of attention. Jenny, who had been number one up till then, was now feeling second best.

Sandra and Rick never wanted things to turn out that way, but a miracle baby changed everything for everyone. Jenny tried to love and bond with her parents and new little brother, but it seemed she was never able to. She saw Michael as a problem and a threat rather than a blessing.

As Jenny and Michael got older, things did get better, but Jenny developed some resentment and started asking questions about being adopted, none of which Sandra could answer. In high school, Jenny started acting out with anger and rage and wanting more attention, causing her parents great concern.

As hard as Sandra tried, she couldn't seem to get Jenny to feel loved as much as Michael.

Jenny eventually graduated from nursing school with honors. Sandra was so proud of her and helped her as much as Jenny would allow her to. Jenny's relationship with Michael became strained, yet she was able to maintain friendly relations with him and seemed to care as much as she possibly could as part of this adoptive family.

Jenny's unanswered questions about her adoption festered over the years and only made her want to know more about her past and why she was abandoned by her birth parent. One day when Jenny was twenty-five, she asked Sandra if she'd go with her to the town where she was born and help her search for answers.

Sandra wholeheartedly agreed and desperately wanted to help her daughter, thinking this was a way they could gain closure for Jenny and grow closer to each other.

Sandra got the name of the hospital and the town where Jenny was born, as well as Jenny's birth name, and off they went on a new adventure. Sandra was happy that Jenny wanted her there as support.

Jenny grew closer to Sandra during their time together researching and tracking down names—it was fun and exciting for them both. Jenny knew her mom loved her enough to come with her on this journey and it felt good.

But the truth isn't always good news. They never thought that what they would discover would be devastating. What they learned changed their lives forever.

During a search at the library for a family with the same last name as her birth parent, Jenny came across the newspaper published during the week she was born. You can get most local news reports from any year, month and date, all on microfilm at local libraries. When she opened the paper, there it was, her birth mother with the headline, "Molly Brown gives birth at thirteen years of age, found murdered." One week later her uncle was arrested for rape, incest, and arranging a murder for hire.

There was a huge media focus on this for months after the news broke, and everyone knew about the murder in that small town. Jenny and Sandra were stunned, shaken to the core. Neither one knew what to say, how to make things right again, or unknow this terrible news. Jenny was angry with Sandra, accused her of knowing the truth all along and withholding it from her, but Sandra was just as shocked as Jenny. Jenny's unreconciled anger found its home directed at Sandra.

The two women drove the five hours back home without speaking; all Jenny could do was cry in anger and hurt. And from then on, Jenny became reclusive. There would be no more coming home for family birthdays, holidays, or even to share a meal; she wanted nothing to do with Sandra, Rick, or Michael.

Sandra and Rick tried for weeks and months to get through to Jenny and show their love and understanding. It broke their hearts to watch helplessly as their daughter slipped further and further into depression. Jenny thought she was severely damaged and beyond repair. She broke off all ties with her friends, coworkers, and a boyfriend and simply stayed in her apartment with no visitors, only answering the phone to say she was okay to her mother, but not allowing visits. She chose to work a night shift at work to stay in her shadowed world.

It broke Sandra's heart, but she continued to reach out to Jenny. After five years, Sandra started experiencing poor health herself and it became harder for her to visit Jenny. Sandra begged her to come over to her house and see her, and finally Jenny did, but said very little and didn't stay long. As Sandra's health deteriorated, Jenny did start feeling remorse about how she had treated her mother, the only mom she ever knew, the only family that never judged her or spoke unkindly about her, the family that did nothing but love her.

As a nurse and caregiver, Jenny loves her job and is very good at it, and though she has very few friends, she is very well-liked by her peers. Jenny is now in her forties and years have passed since she found out the truth about her birth, the answers to the questions of every adopted child. But truth can be tragic.

Jenny is making more of an effort with her family and has returned for more family events and holidays. Though she still doesn't stay very long, at least she knows somewhere in her heart that she is loved and is beginning to try to embrace the family who adopted her and stood by her.

Sandra's story raises questions about how much information adopting parents should seek to know about the children they adopt, and how much should the children be told? I, too, had questions, but accepted my parent's explanations throughout my childhood.

With the encouragement of my family, I made a personal decision to search for my birth mother after both parents had died. I do think children should have their questions answered and that there should not be so much secrecy surrounding their adoptive circumstances.

I believe that all adoption records should be open to adoptive parents and the children they adopt. My hope is that the time of hidden information will change and everyone will have access to the true nature of the adoptive circumstances—good or bad.

I believe that Jenny needed help processing the information she discovered with a professional therapist, but I also know that because Sandra had no way of knowing the truth, she was unable to effectively help her daughter to heal. Jenny chose to process and heal in her own way and in her own time. Jenny had good, kind, and loving parents that had the best intentions when they adopted her. Without knowing everything about a child before adoption, all parents need to be prepared for a battle against the unknown, because most children will ask questions. Unanswered questions drive people to find the truth. All adopted children and their parents need to remember that a family is made from love, respect, and unity and knowing the past will not define you or always help you. "The truth will set you free," is something I have heard all my life. I add to that by saying what you do with that truth will determine if you are really free.

Jenny and her family are finally free, but the truth took a harsh toll on them all.

Tori's Story

Chris and Tori got married on January 1, 2006 and knew they wanted to start a family right away. They tried for almost two years to get pregnant while at the same time pursuing adoption. They reasoned that by pursuing both, God would open a door somewhere. They started the adoption application, but had to put it on hold when Tori became pregnant and gave birth to their first daughter, Tovah, on November 11, 2008.

When Tovah was about a year old, they decided to start the adoption process again, with the intent that the child they adopted would be younger than Tovah. Their adoption application was put on hold again when Tori became pregnant with baby number two. Sadly, their daughter Pat died as an infant of Sudden Infant Death Syndrome and went to heaven to be with Jesus on March 17, 2010.

After grieving the loss of their daughter, they began the adoption process again. This time the family made it all the way through the adoption classes and home study and were waiting to be matched with a child younger than Tovah when they found out they were expecting another baby. Shylee was born June 27, 2011.

When Shylee was about six months old, they returned to the adoption process once again. This time they decided to change their preferences. Instead of looking for a baby or toddler, they decided to pursue an older child. There are thousands of parents waiting to adopt babies, but Tori believed she was called to give a home to an older child waiting to be adopted."

Once they changed their preferences, they completed the adoption process for an older child.

On September 25, 2012, Tori's family was matched with a thirteen-year-old girl in San Antonio named Kambria. Throughout the months of October and November, they drove back and forth from Houston to San Antonio for pre-placement visits with Kambria. Finally, they moved Kambria home to Houston the week of Thanksgiving 2012. As required by law, she lived in their home for six months until the adoption was finalized on June 10, 2013.

There was a lot of adjusting going on, especially in that first year. Though Kambria was never violent toward anyone, she would throw tantrums, screaming and crying to get her way. It was difficult for Chris and Tori as they were trying to parent two toddlers (Tovah was three and Shylee one) and now a teenager who behaved like a toddler. It became increasingly clear that Kambria suffered from emotional disturbances resulting from a lifetime of foster care experiences, and being separated from her from her siblings. After two years, much progress has been made. Her fits have gone from three to four per week, to one every few weeks. Kambria is now fifteen, Tovah six, Shylee three, and Lawrick, their new addition, is three months old. Kambria displays more mature behavior every day. She still expresses social anxiety and has said she doesn't ever want to get married or have children. She repeatedly claims that she will be the crazy cat lady when she grows up—she loves cats. Chris and Tori are just praying that she graduates high school and becomes a productive, contributing member of society.

Kevin and I have known Tori since she was a young teen. She is such a wonderful, caring girl. It has been a joy to see her grow, mature, and marry a wonderful man and enjoy their three biological children and Kambria, their truly special adopted daughter. This story does have a happy ending. But know that adopting at any age is a challenge.

Steve and Mary's Story

From a very young age, Mary wanted to help others. She even thought of being a veterinarian. She grew up thinking of different ways she could make a difference, and always kept that desire to help someone in her heart. As a young woman, she met and married a wonderful, kind and loving man, Steve. Like most newlywed young couples, they talked about having children. Both Mary and Steve wanted children and Mary shared her desire to adopt.

Mary became pregnant three times, losing one baby to miscarriage, and almost losing her third from a serious pregnancy complication that also threatened her own life. Married for ten years, Mary and Steve had two beautiful girls and a loving household, but Mary still had a desire to adopt. They knew they would not have any more of their own children after the youngest was born in such difficult circumstances, and they longed for a boy. So the adoption search began.

They went to friends and family, speaking with people who had adopted children both domestically and from foreign countries. They sought advice from friends and professionals, even considered fostering to adopt. They knew they wanted a newborn to maintain a birth order. Adopting an older child, especially a boy, could bring difficulties to the younger girls as they aged. They chose a domestic adoption and began the process of applying to adopt a child from within the United States.

They wanted background on the birth parents, even to the point of meeting them. They contacted an agency that some friends knew and submitted all the necessary paperwork and a portfolio that would go to birth parents looking for families in which to place their baby. The portfolio contained all the personal information about Mary and Steve and the two girls. Once they were chosen as adoptive parents by the birth parents, Mary and Steve got all the birth mother's information to see if it would be a match for them as well. The family who chose them was married with four children already. This pregnancy was unplanned and they could not afford to raise one more child. It was a difficult decision to give up their son, but both sets of parents felt this was going to work out. The agency did three home visits and submitted mounds of reports before approving the adoption.

Agreements were signed and then the wait began until little Joseph was born. The adoptive parents were responsible for all medical care and aftercare for the birth mother. Mary and Steve were involved in every aspect of the birth, delivery, and all financial support. They spent forty-five thousand dollars after everything was paid for, but they agree that it was all worth it to have their son. They made their decision based on a deep desire to adopt and considered the wisdom and advice of friends and family.

When asked after the adoption process was over what they would like to see change, Steve said he'd like to see changes in how the system handles older, minority children. He'd like to see lower fees, and the encouraging of families to adopt minority children of color into their families.

Sadly, there are more African American children to adopt than children of any other race in our country. Foreign adoptions are harder to complete and more expensive, and obtaining a newborn baby is even harder. Mary and Steve are very happy with their decision, and with an open adoption record, Joseph will be able to know his birth parents when he is older. Mary and Steve stay in touch with the birth parents with letters, gifts, and pictures but no visits until Joseph is ready, they do not want him confused. Too much interaction can confuse a child and even cause abandonment issues, especially since there are other siblings involved. Joseph is a happy little baby with very loving parents and two sisters.

Open adoption isn't for everyone, nor will it always bring you what you expect. If you choose to adopt, explore all your options and find what you think is best for the families and the child. Do not be discouraged in adopting an older child, they can bring much joy to your family, and open adoption will allow you to know everything you can about the child and the birth parents.

Adoption is expensive, so be sure you can afford it, never make a child feel they were difficult to adopt, or that because of adopting, finances are tight, putting guilt on the child. Make them see your love and acceptance and that they are not responsible for the hardships that came in your search for him or her. Your child is a gift, just like your natural children are.

Adopted children everywhere all have a common bond even if we don't know each other; we all know we are different from a biological child raised by his or her birth parents. Many adopted children struggle to feel real acceptance within their adopted family. Many of us miss the feeling of being truly loved and accepted from our birth parents. We know we are cared for, but we only feel detached love because we know we weren't born to be loved the way biological parents raise their newborns.

We usually don't look or act like our adopted families; we have no identity, no genetics, rarely any medical history. That's why we must always discover who and where we come from. It is our right to know and it's a way to heal. Sisters need to know each other, brothers need to know each other, mothers need to know what happened to their children, and children need to know the truth. We always assume the worst, that we weren't loved, and that's why we were given away, and that is very often not the case.

Marcie's Story

I am writing this for various reasons, one being the hope that it will inspire another young woman to choose adoption over abortion. The second, with the hope that it may one day bring me in contact with one or both of the children that I gave up for adoption.

My story starts in the summer between my junior and senior years of high school. I was spending the summer in Seattle, Washington and it was a very wild time in my life. I made several wrong choices and ended up getting pregnant. I do not even know the name of the man by whom I was impregnated, but hope and pray with all my heart that he has come to a happy and saving point of belief in his life. His daughter and I will more than likely never know his identity.

I had returned home to eastern Washington where I was living with my aunt and uncle when I first learned that I was pregnant. I sought the guidance of my Home Economics teacher, whom I was close with, and I am so glad that I did. She instilled in me the value of human life and spared the life of my unborn baby. When I told my aunt and uncle that I was pregnant, they gave me the choice of either having an abortion or moving out. I was adamant that I was not going to abort and decided to give my baby up for adoption. Through the many connections my Home Economics teacher had, I was able to live in a foster home that catered to pregnant teenagers. I was seventeen years old and in my senior year of high school.

I had to leave Deer Park High School to live in that foster home. I missed band; I was the first chair clarinet player at the time. The school I went to while living at the foster home did not have a music program, so I had to give up playing the clarinet. I attended and later graduated from Joseph

Jantsch High School; it was a continuation school for all sorts of troubled teenagers. I was not the only pregnant girl there, which was somewhat comforting.

When it came time for my baby to be born, I had already decided to give her up for adoption. During my pregnancy, I contacted the Hope Adoption Agency and they facilitated the placement of my child for adoption with her new family. I had the great privilege and honor of being able to choose her parents. However, I was not able to meet them because it was considered a closed adoption, which does not permit any personal contact between the birth mother and the adoptive parents. I still have the wrist and ankle bracelets from the hospital that my baby girl had worn while waiting to be taken to her parents.

During the birth, there was a family friend present that helped me choose a name for her—a name I still call her—Sharon Michelle. However, I do know from the adoption agency facilitator that her family named her Victoria and called her Tori. I made the decision to not to hold her in my arms after she was born and do regret this decision because I think that somehow we may have had a stronger connection if I had held her. The reason I gave her up for adoption was because I was so young and didn't think that I was at all ready to be a parent. I later realized that I had made the correct decision for both myself and her at that time in my life. I was very angry then and would possibly have ended up taking that anger out on my child which would have been completely unfair to her. So, for all these years I have hoped and prayed that she had a wonderful life by being raised by her adoptive family. I know that she had an older brother who was also adopted.

This all happened between 1983 and 1984. My baby was

born on May 27, 1984 in Spokane, Washington at Sacred Heart Hospital. For a very long time that was a very special day for me and in my heart I wished her a happy birthday for many years. I have since received inner peace and healing, and no longer feel the pain and sorrow I felt for so many years.

I gave birth to a second child on August 11, 1987. When I got pregnant with her, it was at the same time that I chose to become a Christian, around Thanksgiving of 1986. I was twenty-one when she was born. The relationship I had with her father was very tempestuous, to say the least. We fought a lot and when I told him I was pregnant, he didn't believe he was her father. I knew during the entire pregnancy that I was going to keep her and raise her with or without him in our lives. As it happened, she was three years old before he started seeing her on a regular basis. He never supported her in any way, and never had any sort of relationship with her.

I kept her because I just knew I was supposed to keep her. I did not know her gender until she was born and when I looked into her eyes the very first time while holding her in the hospital I again knew her name was supposed to be Rebecca AnnMarie. I had not had a girl's name picked out previously, only a boy's name.

The third time I got pregnant, I was 23 years old and in a relationship with someone that should have never been in my life in the first place. He ended up signing away his paternal rights when I told him that I had decided to also give this baby up for adoption. She was born on June 9th, 1990. I "named" her Cynthia Rachelle. I sought the assistance of a couple in the church I was going to that did counseling and arranged for a private, closed adoption. I picked out her parents from about three couples that my counselor allowed me to read about. I also have letters from them and her wrist and ankle bands from the hospital. This time I chose to hold her before releasing her to the people that facilitated her adoption. At the time I felt like I could not raise her and my other child all by myself. I later realized that I could have done it, and regretted not raising her. It not only denied me from knowing her but it also denied my daughter that I had chosen to raise from being a big sister to her.

The choices we make at different times in our lives affect not only our lives for all eternity but also the lives of those around us. In this particular instance, the daughter I brought up ended up being raised as an only child even though she had many half-brothers and sisters on her father's side and the two sisters I had given birth to on my side. This has affected her life in innumerable and incalculable ways that none of us may ever know. Thankfully our Lord and Savior knows all and can heal even the deepest wounds caused by our choices.

Today I am happily married to the man I waited forty years for that the Lord kept me for. He has been the absolute model husband and I love him more and more each day. One of the very first things I told him about myself during our first Sunday together was that I had given up two children for adoption and that one day I hoped to be able to find and connect with them in a way that would not be disruptive to them or their families. I still hold the hope that one day we will all be able to connect and form relationships with one another by the grace and love of God.

I can only give this into God's hands for the healing of those deep wounds, and hope and pray that it will touch other people's lives and hearts in some way that may end up saving lives for all eternity.

Robert and Lynette's Story

Robert and Lynette see their sons as blessings. So much so that she says you would never know they weren't birth brothers, they are that close. They were adopted in the US using an adoption placement agency. Robert Junior was five weeks old and Michael came four years later when he was taken at birth from his birth mother. Why they were given up isn't as important to them as where they went, to a loving family who sees them as their own. Lynette says it seems like they were meant to be hers, they have made a family of love and great faith.

Robert and Lynette could not give birth but always knew they would have children. They have a lot of love to give and always wanted to raise children. After finding a reputable agency, the process began.

They both took classes on parenting adoptive children. Lynette said she had to learn how the birth parent feels; she had to step into those shoes to fully understand the gift that was being given to them by a birth parent. Counseling was a big part of the adoption process. With time and patience, their first son was ready for his new parents. They loved Robert Junior from the first time they met him and he bonded with them easily.

In four years, Robert fell in love with his parents and they with him. When the agency notified them that another boy was ready to be born and needed a home, they were thrilled. Robert was going to have a little brother. Robert and Lynette prayed for the birth mother and family during the wait for Jefferey. They remained at the hospital and in the nursery praying. Michael arrived and Lynette, Robert, and Robert Junior were all there to welcome him into their family. It was love at first sight.

The next day Michael went home. Both boys are now teenagers and doing very well in school and sports. It's hard to imagine life without them, Lynette said.

Robert doesn't mind talking about being adopted but Michael is still a bit shy about it; he doesn't see himself as adopted. He just fits in so well that being adopted just doesn't matter. His strong family and faith has made him the wonderful young man he is today.

This testimony brings a happy story to share. Both children have been raised with love, strong Christian faith, and provision. The agency was wonderful to work with and there is no need for the boys to see themselves as adopted, they are simply all family, chosen by God.

Epilogue

Being a mother helped me find something inside me I never knew I had or could give: love, unconditional love. All my fears of being a mother faded away after my sons were born. I made sure they knew what love is and what it wasn't. I can't say I was always mother of the year, but in the eyes of my children, I am. I am at peace with myself. I can love others as well as myself. I know God is for me, so who can be against me? My enemies are few and my friendships are long-lasting. I have had an amazing career; being a mom and a wife, has all been so fulfilling. More than I ever imagined life could be.

I have buried each member of my family except my sons. Life was never lonely but it was different without any family on birthdays, Christmas, Thanksgiving, and other special occasions, but somehow I am always at peace. I longed for family when mine were gone but I had my sons and that was all I really needed. I learned love, acceptance, belonging, and much more through having my own children. I always wanted to adopt and give a child what they may not have, but somehow the timing was never right.

Orphans will always be in my heart and prayers. My desire is that every child never goes to sleep feeling unloved like I did.

During a mission trip to Honduras, I saw children begging late at night in the streets, hungry, cold, dirty, no extra clothes, unloved or cared for, and with nowhere to live. It broke my heart into a million pieces, I cried for days and weeks for those lost children. The thought of them not being loved really got to me. I shared my feelings with Kevin and he felt the same way. During our second visit, I knew something had to be done. I couldn't rescue all of them but we could help some. When we returned, after talking with a pastor and his wife in Honduras, we spoke with our pastor, Rick Minett, at our home church. He was excited to take a crew to Honduras to build an orphanage there and get it ready to take in ten kids.

It was no easy task, but love always prevails. We would love to see more help come to the children of the streets and to all orphans in the US and other countries. I continue to pray for them all as well as weep for them to be saved from getting hurt, or starving. I have seen love in action and it is so exciting! I want all people to know love and belonging. We all are gifted with different talents. I encourage everyone to pay it forward in your daily life and give the best gift of all, love.

Appendix

References

Adoption and tax credits:
https://www.irs.gov/taxtopics/tc607.html

Adoption Basics and facts:
www.ccainstitute.org,
www.journeychristiannews.com

Adoption Basics

People search for love, sometimes in all the wrong places. Some search through songs, poems, stories, or through others, but really, love has to be in you first, loving who you are is paramount to loving others deeply. As a child, love needs to be shown, felt, taught, experienced, but if it isn't, it is up to that child to search for that need to be fulfilled. That is why life is a journey, always searching, always learning along the way.

Sometimes life will throw you a curve or a road block, but be persistent to find what you need. I don't think you ever reach an end to this journey because we should always be open to learn and grow in our hearts and minds.

Adoption isn't for everyone, nor will it bring you what you expected. But if you are willing to really love the way I have explained, then maybe you should adopt. However, if you really cannot overlook a child's differences and you are only in love with your husband and your life without children, then maybe adoption is not for you.

Consider what you are able to handle, make sure you are not self-seeking, or just want to try parenting, or your clock is ticking and the pressure is on to have children. Never adopt for any reason other than really being able and wanting to love at all times and seek the best of that child no matter what heartache they may bring. Ask yourself, "Can I really unconditionally love a child that I did not give birth to?"

Vera was put in a situation she was not prepared for, could you have loved Hermine as your own? I am not sure even I could. I do not blame anyone for my life's struggles but I am grateful for the truth I found, and the love I learned through having my own children. The purpose of adoption should always be love, make a checklist from your heart. If you cannot pass the love test, do not adopt. Lives depend on it.

We must adopt from an unselfish heart, a heart that can love a child through everything that comes, look for the good, and not blame them because of bad genes or because they were not birthed by you. Love will grow if it is fed properly.

Adoptions can be open or closed. Open adoption allows for communication between the adoptive and biological parents. In some jurisdictions, the biological and adoptive parents may enter into legally enforceable agreements in the adoption process. It is wise to have assistance from a lawyer when preparing these contracts.

Closed, confidential, or secret adoption, involves the sealing of all identifying information between the sets of parents.

Adoptions can occur between related or unrelated people. A common example is a stepparent adoption of a child from a spouse's previous relationship. Common law adoption permits parents to leave children with friends or relatives for extended periods, after which some courts recognize the voluntary cohabitation as binding. In these situations, assistance from a knowledgeable lawyer is a good idea. Each state may have different laws, do your research.

In private, domestic adoptions, charities and businesses serve prospective adoptive parents and families who want to place children. Private adoption accounts for a large number of adoptions; the United States Department of Health & Human Services estimates that nearly 45% of adoptions in the US are private.

Terminated Adoptions

Not every adoption has a storybook ending. The processes of terminating adoptions are called disruption and dissolution. Disruption takes place before an adoption is finalized, while dissolution takes place afterwards. Studies by the Child Welfare Information Gateway suggest that 10% to 25% of adoptions disrupt, and 1% to 10% dissolve. Adoptive parents initiate these processes through court petitions that resemble divorce. In these types of situations, it is a good idea to seek help from a lawyer who is familiar with these less-than-fortunate placements.

Identity

As an aspiring adoptive parent, it is important to realize that many adopted children experience difficulty in establishing their sense of identity. Identity takes form in early childhood, and family relationships are important to its development and outcome. By the time children start school, they ask questions about who they are, where they belong, and how they fit into the family. These questions can be complicated for adopted children and adoptive parents. During these conversations, it can be beneficial to have the help of a therapist who understands family dynamics and the emotional needs of your child.

Adoption needs to be looked at very carefully, pros and cons. Ask yourself if you could really love a child you did not give birth to? If that child caused you lots of problems, became mentally ill, or had defects and health issues, could you lay down your life for that child? How far would you be willing to love? Not all children become a blessing to their parents, and that includes natural children as well as adopted. If you did not come from a loving home, will you be able to give what you never had? Would you be willing to pay thousands, take parenting classes, and wait six months or several years to adopt a child? Would you take an older child, or are babies easier to love? What are your needs and requirements for a child to be loved and accepted in your family? If you adopt for any of the wrong reasons, you may grow to regret it and even become abusive if the child turns out very different than you expected. Then what will you do?

Every child deserves to be loved, accepted, and cared for. Provision is required and easier to give but love has to come from your heart. Provision is on the top of the list of adopting both pets and children, but why is love not the main requirement? When a family adopts and the parents get a divorce, how will that child feel? You better have a strong marriage and love in that marriage, because you can't give out what you do not have. Your love tank has to stay full! If it runs on empty, you may never survive being an adoptive parent. Find joy in everything, even if your child acts up, love will always turn things around. I know parents who wanted to give up in a marriage, and some have; then what happens to that child? If you and your spouse are headed toward divorce, adopting a child to save a marriage is a wrong reason to adopt in my opinion. Also, if you are already divorced and feeling lonely, adopting a child may not fill the void, but adopting a pet might.

Adoption Facts

Quotes from Journey Christian news publication and (www.ccainstitute.org)

According to the US State Department, there were over 7,000 children adopted into US families in 2012, and an additional 104,000 children are in foster care awaiting adoption.

There are 53 million estimated orphans worldwide, and these numbers are increasing each year.

Adoption in the US has a pattern of being impacted directly by what was happening in the world:

- 1850s: the first modern adoption law was passed in Massachusetts

- 1940s: just after World War II, the practice of international adoptions increased

- 1950 –1953: the Korean War spurred the beginning of the largest wave of international adoptions worldwide.

- Between 1950 and 2000, South Korea expedited the adoption of over 150,000 Korean children to the US and

50,000 in Europe, Canada and Australia.

- 1970s: the Vietnam war caused another increase with the controversial "Operation Baby Lift" when over 2,000 children, many thought to be fathered by American GI's, were brought to the US in a much publicized humanitarian rescue, and all of them were adopted.
- 1991: US families adopted over 2,000 Romanian children
- 2000: adoption from China increased, over 20,000 Chinese children, mostly girls, were adopted in the US

Types of Adoption

Open Adoption

An open adoption is when an adoptive family and the birth family keep in contact for the benefit of a child. Contact in an open adoption can mean different things to different families as contact can range from letters and emails, to phone calls, or regular visitation. It all rests on the adults to create a plan that fits everyone's needs and expectations.

An open adoption can be arranged in domestic adoptions including foster care adoption. Birth family contact can include birth parents, grandparents, and/or siblings. There have even been cases of open adoptions in international adoptions.

As is the case with many decisions in life, there are pros and cons to choosing an open adoption.

Pros of an Open Adoption

Answers to the big question - Since the adoptees will have

some contact with the birth family, they may not have the feeling of "missing a piece" which some adoptees have stated having. They will also have the opportunity to ask the big question, "Why was I placed for adoption?" The need to fantasize or romanticize birth family circumstances is then removed from the equation and the adopted child can grow up with truth and knowing birth parents.

- Link to heritage and ancestry - The adoptees within an open adoption will also have access to background on their heritage, ancestry, medical history. They will be able to claim that information as a piece of their identity.

- Wider circle of family and support - The adoptee within an open adoption may have more family to provide love, support, and historical information. The adoptive family may also be grateful for the extra support provided by the birth parents who love their child.

- Medical information readily available - Many adoptees lack access to basic medical background information. This information can be vital to helping medical personnel and adoptive parents make informed decisions on behalf of the children. This valuable information also pertains to mental and emotional health.

- No need to search - Many adoptees do not know the details of their birth or adoption story. As they grow older, an adoptee in an open adoption will have this information, and will not have to suffer through an adoption search. Adoption searches can exhaust a person emotionally and financially.

Cons of an Open Adoption

- Possible boundary issues - Some birth families may

struggle with knowing how they fit into the big picture as the child grows. While they may be actively involved in their child's life, the adoptive family provides a sense of stability. Adoptive families may struggle with knowing how to incorporate two sets of parents into the child's life.

This is understandable, but can be managed. Communicate up front what the boundaries are in regards to visitation, phone calls, and birth parent input in the raising of the child. And remember that everything can be renegotiated as the child grows up.

- Unrealistic expectations - Unmet expectations can be an issue on both sides of an open adoption. A birth parent may expect perfection from an adoptive parent, while an adoptive parent may expect the birth parent to play a quieter role in their child's life. This is why it's important to establish expectations and boundaries at the very beginning of the relationship. While expectations and boundaries may change, your child's need for stability will not.

- Exposure by the birth parents to those with whom the adoptive family would not normally associate - It may sound ugly, but who the birth family associates with can be a serious factor. We all have our own morals and values, and not everyone agrees on lifestyle choices. Most people choose their friends based on many different factors. What if birth parents and adoptive parents just don't mesh well? Consider what is best for the child over your own needs first.

- Safety - If it's a matter of safety, such as drug use, then limit contact to letters or emails, but explain that change to the other party and to the adoptee. Often in the case of foster care adoptions, the child was removed for their safety. Safety should always be the number one priority.

Consider how the cons seem to be about the communication and social issues between adoptive and birth parents while the pros are all a possible benefit to the adoptee and point to the overall best interests of the child. Isn't that what most of us are here for--to provide for a child? Please keep these things in mind when considering an open adoption.

If you are having a tough time making a decision on whether or not to choose an open adoption, consult an adoption specialist such as a social worker or therapist who will become familiar with your family. Foster care is used when a child's needs are not provided for or in cases of abuse or neglect in the home that affect the safety of the child. Prospective adopting families often file to adopt through the foster care system. This process is lengthy and extensive, so you will need to be prepared and know it will take time and energy. Children leave the foster care system at eighteen years of age—also referred to as opting out. Unfortunately after eighteen, most children aren't prepared to take full responsibility for themselves and fall into the hands of society on their own. They have not been fully prepared by the foster care system to become a responsible citizen and live in the world as an adult. They often become products of a broken system. In many locations, these now "adult children" receive no resources, support, money, home or anything else to prepare them to be an adult on their own. They often end up in homeless shelters or jail, but some also succeed.

Legal/Closed Adoption

This is the most widely used system for adopting a child. There are many agencies you can use to find a child that you are seeking. Make sure the agency is accredited—check them out thoroughly through a law firm that specializes in adoption or through the foster care system; they can recommend a good agency. The fees can be high, especially if you want a newborn and have to pay for the birth and birth mother's expenses. Make sure you are prepared for all expenses and get as much information as possible about the child and birth parents. Foreign adoptions are even more costly, so be prepared.

Surrogate Adoption

If either of the adoptive parents is sterile, surrogate adoption is an option. A surrogate birth is one in which adoptive parents pay to have a donor egg or sperm (could be known or unknown father) placed in surrogate woman's womb to carry their child to full term. As you can imagine, this can be tricky business. Although it sounds loving and caring, it has presented difficulties. This agreement needs to be entered through legal counsel. Once the baby is born, the surrogate mother might get attached and change her mind or want to be involved in the baby's life, and that could cause the child to grow up with some confusion. It is wonderful to be involved in your child's birth, but would you be prepared if things went very wrong?

Recently, I met a woman who agreed to be a surrogate and carry a child for a childless couple she had never met and who lived in another state. She had two children of her own and always felt good being pregnant, yet she didn't want to raise anymore of her own. So she and her husband went on the internet searching for a couple who was looking for a surrogate to carry their child. She met with the couple via Skype, and maintained contact through email, on the phone, and through their lawyer. An agreement was made that she would turn over the baby at birth to the adoptive couple.

The adoptive father donated his sperm and the surrogate mother provided her egg, both of which were implanted in the surrogate mother. All costs were covered by the adoptive couple. In the beginning of the fourth month of pregnancy, the surrogate became very tired, more than she thought was normal. An ultrasound was taken and she found she was pregnant with twins. Wow, that was a shock to everyone. Her care became much more expensive and she had to quit work and go on bed rest in her fifth month. This was very hard on her and she could not travel to have the babies in the same state with the adoptive couple, so they had to fly out in the ninth month to stay near the surrogate. The final expenses far exceeded any predictions—after all, it was now a high-risk birth carrying twins. After the cesarean section surgery and recovery from the birth, the surrogate mother wanted to hold the babies before they were turned over to the adoptive parents. Once she held the babies close to her, she felt she had made a mistake and didn't want to give them up, but she had already entered into a legal and binding agreement. Now this happy event turned into great sadness for the surrogate and her family.

I personally think this method of adopting a child is very costly and complicated. I am not totally sure people are fully prepared for this method of having a child, even if they have obtained significant counseling in preparation for what should be one of the happiest moments in life.

Additional topics to consider

If at all possible, gather all the information you can before you adopt and get everything in a legal binding agreement. I suggest that you inform, in a kind and loving way, your child at an appropriate age that they were adopted. Never withhold that, because one day they will find out, and it could damage your family and cause great harm in the areas of trust between you and your child.

I was told at a very young age that I was adopted. I was told I was saved from a terrible life and a teenage mother who could not care for me. I was always introduced to other people as "the adopted daughter." I was told I needed to be grateful for everything my adoptive parents had provided me. It is true, my parents provided for me. I had food, nice places to live, education, and all my needs were met. I guess you could say I had provision. What I was missing was love, that comes from a very different place, a place in someone's heart, and that can't be purchased. I didn't really learn that till I was in love with my own children.

Welcoming a child into your family doesn't always involve a trip to the delivery room or any traditional aspects of giving birth. Sometimes it requires thorough research, assistance from a lawyer, and visits from adoption officials. Domestic adoption is an option that thousands of aspiring parents in the United States pursue every year. Before you decide to adopt from inside US borders, do your homework.

I was adopted for the wrong reasons. I never felt loved, but I did feel provided for. Was provision enough? No it was not. I longed for love and acceptance. It took me over thirty-three years to really understand how love works. When my children were born, I was in awe of how I gave birth to these two beautiful boys, yet I had to learn how to love them, teach them, and provide for them. I was scared to death. I had to learn how to love because no one showed me that kind of love.

I am grateful that my needs were met, but the hole in my heart grew larger and, over time, was never filled till I learned about God's love for me. That is the love I was after. That is the love I was seeking all my life.

Adoption is a very serious decision, take time, do research, and always search your heart about it.

One more thing I just heard of a few years ago; re-homing of adopted children. Apparently parents are sending their adoptive children off to live with another family because they changed their minds, or parenting was not what they thought it would be, and the child didn't turn out to fit in. I gathered information that stated an adoptive parent can search for a family, interview them, and arrange a place to meet and turn over the child to another family. All without even knowing them.

I believe this will cause great harm to any child. I find this method deplorable and it should be illegal. I have heard of some extreme cases that really upset me. A child already has conflicting feelings about being adopted and abandoned; adding more by giving them over to strangers takes it to the level of being abusive and irresponsible. You can rehome a pet, but not a child!

I am a pet lover and have adopted several in my life. I have seen an increase in the shelters and rescue organizations to find animals a good, loving home. The screening process is extensive and there is a fee when you do adopt. Once you take your pet home, the likelihood is that no one will check up on your care for that animal.

I hoped our child adoption system would be much better than this. After adopting a child, he or she should be checked on for at least the first year. I do think there is more awareness about adopting and I think there is still a lot more that can be learned and done. Some people do take better care of their pets than they do their children and some people are just mean to both. I think children are our most precious gift, parents have a huge responsibility to take care of children they adopt; to teach and show love, not just till a child is eighteen and/or moves out, but for a lifetime. Your job as a parent doesn't end when they become an adult. As much as I treasure the experience and memories of my children growing up, moving out, and taking care of themselves, my love and concern never has ended. Both of my boys stayed at home till they were twenty. Now I wish they hadn't grown up so fast, but we do remain very close.

Adoption has the power to transform a life. It comes with its ups and downs, but with good parenting, love, and an opportunity to thrive, an adopted child has a better chance than those who are left to orphanages or the streets.

The desire to save a life is an honorable thing, but ask yourself if realistically you are able to handle it, both financially and emotionally through all the highs and lows, through serious illnesses, birth defects, or mental illness. Most children come with very little known about them, records are still closed in many countries including most of the U.S. In Austria, I was allowed to look at the records but not copy or even photograph them. The information I got there was just verification of what was in my documents, no health records or family history. Even my birth mother didn't have her family medical history because she was estranged from them at age 16. There was no way I could walk out with anything pertaining to my birth records or about both birth parents. I strongly believe these hidden records need to be brought into the light in every state and nation.

Now with so many ways to adopt a child, records are vital. I never knew about genetics or the history of any parent. So many things are connected with genetics and origin, and not being able to know can often be a health danger either in the child or the child's children. Genetics are after all passed down from generation to generation. It is necessary to get as much information as possible. In Third World countries, nutrition plays a huge part in a child's health, as do genetics. Many women are raped or forced to marry relatives as well as much older men. Any child born from such conditions might be at a higher risk. Many people who want to help these children are often misled about the birth conditions of these children.

Churches have been known to rescue orphans. In ancient Roman days, children were discarded or the Romans would choose to kill their own children rather than face the difficulties of raising them. Children today continue to be victimized by the selfish lifestyles of their parents. Many abusive parents become that way out of frustration and demands of raising children. Often there are too many children in a home and the parents just cannot care for all of them. Sometimes a parent will commit suicide or kill their own as a way out. Perhaps adoption could have saved some of these children.

There are thousands of children removed from abusive parents and put in the foster care system today. Often they are returned to their abusive parents because the courts think they are better off with a birth parent than to be in the system. And often the abuse only stops after the child dies, ends up in the hospital, a parent is taken to jail, or the child grows up and leaves the home. What is their future?

People need to be educated, aware of all these facts and be informed before adopting. As children grow up and develop their own character, many become what they have been taught or witnessed. Also affecting their outcome is what they discover along the way from just being exposed to different groups of people. I believe hate is taught along with anger, selfishness, abuse, wrong or right ways, even language that is spoken in the home, not just English but cursing and praising. We live in a world of free speech but that does not mean we don't need to teach self-control.

REFLECTIONS

Vera & Lloyd McDaniel, Fayetteville, NC

Lt. LLoyd McDaniel
US Army

Vera McDaniel

Hairdresser Finds Her Roots

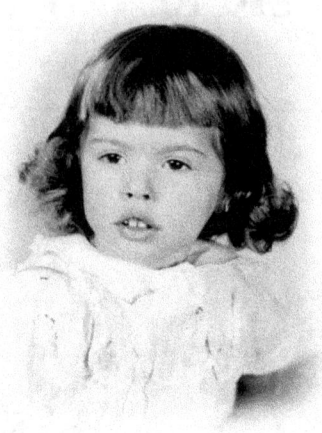

Hermine, Illinois, 1952

```
C O P Y
M 4587/49-Schei/W                    Salzburg, 30 Jan 1951
Re: minor Matejovits Hermine


                    D e c l a r a t i o n.


        As the unmarried mother of the child, born on 12 June
1949, I herewith give my irrevocable consent to the adoption
of this child by adoptive parents from Venezuela to be chosen,
and abandon my maternal rights entirely in favor of the adoptive
parents.

        I also give my consent to the emigration of the child to
Venezuela.


In my presence:                  Sign.: Matejovic Gertrud e.h.
Sign.Scheichl e.h.

                    Town Council of Salzburg
                        Youth Commission
                                          Round official stamp:
F.d.R.d.A.                                Town Council of
Stamp:                                    Salzburg, Court for
Youth Commission of the Town              the protection of
Salzburg, Office f.Guardianship           wards.
```

The adoption paper Gertrud never signed

Reflections

City view of Salzburg

Geburtsurkunde

(Standesamt) — — — — — Salzburg — — — — — Nr. 1043/49

— — — — — — — Hermine Anna Matejovic — — — — — — —

ist am 12. Juni 1949 um 19 Uhr 30 Minuten — — — — — — —

in Salzburg, Müllner Hauptstraße Nr. 48 — — — — — geboren.

Mutter: Gertrud Matejovic, Hilfsarbeiterin, katholisch, — —

wohnhaft in Salzburg, Linzergasse Nr. 15 — — — — — — —

Änderungen der Eintragung: Das Kind führt zufolge Adoption vom 15.
Juni 1951 durch die Eheleute Lloyd Leslie Mc Daniel und Vera,
geborene Brown, den Familiennamen " Mc D a n i e l " — — — —

— —

Salzburg — — — — —, den 15. Oktober — — 1951

Der Standesbeamte
In Vertretung:

Zerger

Ostermiething Sept. 24th, 94

Dear Hermine & Family !!!

My dear daughter, I'm your real, physical mother from Austria in fact.
I was very pleased about your letter and the photos.
I thank you with all one's heart that you have been looking for me.
I've been trying to seek after you with the help of the Austrian Red Cross Organisation - without success.

I'm so happy that you and your 2 lovely children are well and that you've got such a good, nice husband.

I'm very glad to have heard that you had a nice childhood.
Terrible circumstances have lead you to adoptive parents.
I really do hope you'll understand that I'm not able to explain everything in one letter and you canbelieve me how worried I've been those times about you and your faith.
I'm going to tell you everything honestly step by step in the letters following.

First letter from Gertrud to Mickee
confirming their
mother/daughter relationship

Reflections

Let us primarilly be happy that we've found each other again !!

I've been sick now for one year. My little toe (right foot) has been amputated and a vein-byepass has been put into my thigh but it's still getting a bit better. I can hardly walk therefore.

I've been a widow for 22 years.
Mr. KAINER and me - we've been married for 15 years - were sailors (river-shipping) until he was killed in an accident.

Since 6 years I've made friends with a very nice man - you can see him on the photo together with me - He tries to give all the best for me.

I was born on March 16th, 1931 in SALZBURG - you have been born there, too, my dear daughter-

Now I'm 63 years old.
Your dad was an American soldier and the first man in my life. I suppose that's the reason why you`re that pretty and somebody extra special.
I love you with all one's heart and with all my life !

We've rent a little house in the country and we've been living there since all allone.

Because I've had a uterus (womb) operation I was not able to get children after.

But now I've got **YOU**!

You are a kind of **GOD**'s present for me.

I'm still able to speak and read little English but I've got problems at writing it.
In my circle of acquaintances there are some people who help to translate my words into English.

Now I'm waiting with ardent desire for an answer!

Thousand kisses and greetings to you, your 2 boys and to your husband.

Yours you ever loving **Mum** !!!!!!

About the Author

Mickee is a hairdresser in Hendersonville, North Carolina where she is a friend to everyone, sharing a smile, a boisterous "hello" or a hand to someone in need. *Hairdresser Finds Her Roots* is her first book, one that started because dozens of people throughout her adult life told her that she needs to share her story with the world.

Mickee's optimism is remarkable and contagious. She tells the story with stark honesty taking you from laughter to holding your breath from chapter to revealing chapter as her unbelievable story unfolds.

What best qualifies Mickee to write this book is her great love for children—she and Kevin continue to support the orphanage in Honduras that they founded—and her trust in humanity; that we can all rise up to be the best of ourselves in our families and in our communities.

www.ingramcontent.com/pod-product-compliance
Lightning Source LLC
Chambersburg PA
CBHW062038120526
44592CB00035B/1245